RENEWING
YOUR
SPIRITUAL
LIFE

A STUDY OF DEUTERONOMY:
13 Simple Steps for Maximum Spiritual Growth

RENEWING YOUR SPIRITUAL LIFE

A STUDY OF DEUTERONOMY:
13 Simple Steps for Maximum Spiritual Growth

by

AUBREY JOHNSON

Gospel Advocate Company
Nashville, Tennessee

Published by Gospel Advocate Co.
1006 Elm Hill Pike, Nashville, TN 37210
http://www.gospeladvocate.com

ISBN: 0-89225-546-3

DEDICATION

This book is dedicated to Lisa my wife, best friend and partner in the continual quest for spiritual renewal.

ACKNOWLEDGEMENTS

I want to express my gratitude to Dr. Rodney Cloud for his commitment to Old Testament scholarship and a wonderful class on the book of Deuteronomy. Thanks to Clyde Miller, Marge Landrum and the Gospel Advocate editorial department for proofreading the text. I especially appreciate the elders and members of the Eastside Church of Christ in Duncan, Okla., for their support while I worked on this manuscript in conjunction with teaching the material in class. Most of all, I want to thank my friend Mary Thurman for her enthusiastic support of this book and her belief in my promise as a writer.

TABLE OF CONTENTS

INTRODUCTION

Is spiritual renewal the private domain of monks and mystics? No way! God wants all of His children to experience the joy of being inwardly renewed day by day (2 Corinthians 4:16). Are you ready to cross over the mental and emotional barriers that have halted your spiritual progress in the past? Are you prepared to take a giant leap forward in your relationship with God? Then this book will provide you with the practical help you have been looking for to revive your spiritual life. Although commitment is required, you will be surprised to discover just how simple sanctification can be.

Before getting started, let me encourage you to pause for a moment of prayer. Ask God to open your heart and mind to His will. Ask Him to help you internalize the lessons and translate them into action. Ask Him to refresh your soul and renew your spirit. As you pray, remember God's promise: "Ask, and it will be given to you; seek, and you will find; knock, and it will be opened to you" (Matthew 7:7). With this assurance in mind, let the transformation begin!

Background

When Israel was preparing to enter the Promised Land, Moses revealed a secret that would guarantee the people military victory, economic prosperity and spiritual vitality. That secret was to honor God's covenant. Those who follow Moses' advice find that it still works today! Simply put, renewal is the result of committed love for God and obedience to His Word. This book will show you how to apply this principle in a variety of day-to-day settings. Moses' appeal for covenant faithfulness was preserved in Deuteronomy, and that book will serve as the launching point for each lesson in this study. The primary focus, however, will be on New Testament parallels drawn from the life and teaching of Jesus.

This book is about daily spiritual renewal for Christians and not a commentary on Deuteronomy. Still, familiarity with that Old Testament book can enrich your study of this material. Deuteronomy was written under special circumstances and in a style unlike anything else in the Bible. This section is a little more technical than the rest of the book, but it isn't long, and it will greatly benefit your understanding and enjoyment of what follows. Wade in and witness God's amazing plan for renewing His people.

Name

Deuteronomy is the fifth and final book written by Moses and the premier Old Testament text on the subject of renewal. The title is derived from the Greek (Septuagint) translation of Deuteronomy 17:18 and means "second law." The word "second" refers to the communication of the law rather than its content. Moses' aim was not to provide a new and distinct body of teaching different from what he delivered earlier at Sinai. Rather, his intent was to restate the same law and urge the Israelites to reaffirm it.

Classification

Deuteronomy is not a detailed law code like Leviticus or a historical narrative like most of Genesis, Exodus and Numbers. It is a record of spoken addresses preserved in the literary form of ancient covenant documents. The Hebrew Bible is known for deriving a book's title from the first words of the first line of text. According to this method, the name for Deuteronomy is "these are the words." That label is appropriate because the book consists of a written record of three farewell speeches from Moses to the Israelites.

Overview

In his first message, Moses retraced what God did for Israel during its brief but glorious history (chapters 1-4). The second message concentrated on the commandments given by the Lord to bless His covenant people (chapters 5-26). In the third address, Moses explained the blessings and curses connected with the law to encourage the Israelites to obey it (chapters 27-28). A final charge for faithfulness was given by Moses before the book closed with an account of the prophet's death (chapters 29-34).

Setting

Those who read Deuteronomy need to familiarize themselves with the setting of the book to enhance their appreciation of these speeches. From the plains of Moab east of the Jordan, the travel-weary Israelites gazed across the river to the land of milk and honey awaiting them. Before the conquest of Canaan could begin, their leader had something important to say. Moses is pictured as a powerful preacher warning, advising and encouraging his congregation.

Moses desperately wanted to prepare the people for the difficulties he knew they would face. To accomplish his purpose, the nation would hold two special assemblies to seal their covenant with God: one before entering Canaan and a second after initial victories secured the land. The first covenant-renewal ceremony was taking place as Moses spoke. The latter would occur at Shechem where, centuries earlier, Jacob built an altar and worshiped the Lord (Joshua 8). In the shadow of Mount Ebal to the north and Mount Gerizim to the south, the Israelites would reaffirm the covenant and acknowledge that their victory over the Canaanites was because of God's power rather than their own military might and genius. The ceremony would also remind them that future battles must be waged on the same wholehearted commitment to God that brought past success. Because the final chapter includes an account of the death of Moses, it is possible that the present form of the book contains contributions by Joshua around the time of the latter ceremony.

Theme

Moses told the Israelites that he would not be allowed to enter the new land with them. Joshua would succeed him, but more important was the promise of God's presence as they undertook battle against the armies of Canaan. In actuality, there was no change in leadership, only in human representation. To the people, Moses and the covenant may have seemed inseparable, but he was merely the first in a long line of distinguished prophets who communicated the words of their true leader, God.

The Israelites had no reason to fear as long as they were faithful to their covenant with the Lord. If they returned God's love by obeying Him, they could expect a prosperous life in Canaan. If they disobeyed the laws God designed to benefit them, they would reap devastating consequences. The theme underlying each of Moses' sermons was the importance of absolute commitment to God.

Deuteronomy is filled with relevance for contemporary Christians. Quoted more than 80 times in the New Testament in 21 different books, its message is a model for the church in today's changing culture. Like the Israelites before them, Christians need to commit themselves wholeheartedly to the Lord.

Treaty Form

In recent years, scholars have recognized striking similarities between Deuteronomy and treaties between Near Eastern kings of the second millennium and their vassals. A typical treaty would contain: (1) a preamble identifying the king, (2) a historical prologue evoking memories of past events that form the basis of the covenant and inspire obedience to it, (3) stipulations outlining the responsibilities of the covenant relationship, (4) sanctions, both positive and negative, to encourage loyalty, and (5) witnesses who would carry out the appropriate sanctions.

This treaty form is evident in Deuteronomy. Israel had been the vassal of pharaohs in Egypt, but following the exodus, the people were free to serve the Lord. They could accept or reject the covenant initiated by God, but it was not open to negotiation. God was king, and the covenant was His constitution. As their savior and protector, He deserved the allegiance of His people.

As a member of Egypt's royal family, Moses received a superior education (Acts 7:21-22), including instruction in foreign affairs. It is not surprising then that Moses' words in Deuteronomy seem to follow the pattern of political treaties of his day. This plan appears to be more than a literary device. Israel, as a theocracy, was actually reaffirming its covenant with God as suzerain. Note the resemblances between Deuteronomy and the style of vassal treaties contemporary with the time in which it was written:

Preamble 1:1-5
Historical Prologue 1:6-4:43
Stipulations 4:44-26:19
Sanctions 27:1-28:68
Witness 30:19; 31:19; 32:1-43

The discovery of this treaty form demonstrates not only the early date of Deuteronomy but also the importance of Israel's covenant-relationship with God. Readers are witnesses to a covenant-renewal ceremony between the Lord and His people. A similar agreement had been entered into at Sinai by an earlier generation, but they chose the road of disobedience and perished in the desert. Their fate in the wilderness was a warning to all who would come after them. God demands more than a mere declaration of loyalty. The lives of His people must bear out the profession of their faith. The treaty God made with Israel at Sinai was never intended to be restricted to one generation. It was the commencement of a continuing relationship spanning countless generations. The time had arrived for the descendants of those who died in the desert to decide what they would do regarding the covenant. Like their predecessors, they had to make a choice. Life, liberty and happiness all depended on choosing loving obedience to God.

Preamble

The first five verses of Deuteronomy form the preamble to the entire book. Moses is identified as the spokesperson of the Lord. His prophetic role foreshadowed the emergence of a greater prophet on the nation's horizon. Jesus fulfilled the role of Moses by initiating the New Covenant with spiritual Israel. He was not only "the Prophet" like unto Moses whose coming was predicted in Deuteronomy 18 but the incarnate King himself who spoke His own words (vv. 15, 18).

Moses' audience was "all Israel" (Deuteronomy 1:1), and the place where he spoke was "on this side of the Jordan in the wilderness," referring to the eastern side of the river. Several locations mentioned cannot be identified with certainty today. Horeb is used to designate the general area in which Sinai is found and may be used as a synonym for the famous mountain.

The renewal of the covenant took place at the beginning of the 11th month of the 40th year of wilderness wandering after the exodus from Egypt. It is only an 11-day journey from Horeb to Kadesh Barnea where the Israelites were originally supposed to launch the conquest of Canaan. Moses contrasted that brief journey with the 40 years of roaming that resulted from their unwillingness to trust and obey God.

The preamble clarifies that Moses' words were not his own. He spoke "all that the Lord had given him in commandment to them" (Deuteronomy 1:3). It was a new day, and God was giving a new generation of Israelites an opportunity to complete the unfulfilled mission of their parents. In victories over Sihon and Og, they tasted sweet success guaranteed to continue if they relied on the Lord.

With this in mind, Moses began to "declare" (Deuteronomy 1:5 KJV) God's instructions to the people. The Hebrew word for "declare" means to make something completely clear. Translated in Deuteronomy 27:8 as "very plainly" (KJV), it described the legibility with which the laws of God were inscribed in stone. Moses sought to engrave God's words on the heart of every Israelite.

Moses did much more than passively provide information. He passionately explained the meaning of God's law and urged the people to obey it. The intensity with which he spoke evidenced his genuine love for God and man. Moses knew that understanding and keeping this law were the basis for preserving Israel's covenant relationship with God and receiving the blessings it afforded. As we shall see, faith and obedience remain the foundation of spiritual renewal today.

1

RENEW YOUR LOVE
"An Offer You Cannot Refuse"

Are you experiencing the spiritual blahs? Do you find yourself just going through the motions in worship? Are you confident God exists yet don't feel close to Him anymore? If you answered "yes" to any of these questions, then you need renewing! This book is devoted to promoting spiritual renewal in the lives of people desiring new heights of holiness. If you feel stuck, if you have reached a plateau, if you would like to accelerate your spiritual growth, then this book can rekindle the fire in your soul.

> **Encouragement for Renewal**
>
> *If I am to know spiritual renewal, I must renew my covenant with God.*

"Renewal" is the word used to describe a positive change in a person's relationship with God. The term describes the process of reviving or repairing something that has faded from its earlier glory. In a spiritual context, it implies that ties to God have grown weak and call for restoration. Whether your faith needs freshening or a complete overhaul, you will be provided with the practical tools you need to get the job done.

This book is short and simple by design. Its basic premise is that spiritual renewal is not a mysterious and complicated process. It all comes down to two things – loving God and keeping His commandments. If you are seriously committed to becoming a more spiritual person, then read on.

Handicapped Souls

Just as physical life begins at conception, so does spiritual life. The life-giving seed is the Word of God (1 Peter 1:23). When it is planted in a receptive heart, a conversion process begins that brings about the spiritual birth that occurs at baptism. As new Christians grow, they feed upon the milk of God's Word (2:2). In time, that milk is replaced by meatier teachings suitable to a higher state of maturity (1 Corinthians 3:2). The ultimate goal is to grow into the likeness of the Lord (Ephesians 4:13).

Unfortunately, just as the human body may experience slow or abnormal development, so can the spirit. Many Christians are spiritually handicapped and do not realize it. Their prayer life is stale. Their knowledge is shallow. Their motives are selfish. The good news is that the condition underlying these disturbing symptoms can be corrected. All that is needed is desire.

Covenant Relationships

The Bible uses a variety of metaphors to highlight different parts of God's multifaceted personality. He is alternately pictured as a shepherd, father, husband, potter, gardener and warrior. The principal image used by Moses in Deuteronomy was that of a benevolent king. Renewal, therefore, is comparable to the restoration of healthy ties between a merciful monarch and his people. In ancient times, when a king controlled a new territory, he made a covenant with its citizens. This written agreement would accomplish several things:

1. It would identify the new lord of the land.

2. It would inspire loyalty by recalling what the king had done in their behalf.

3. It would set forth the expectations of those entering the covenant.

4. It would explain the consequences of keeping or breaking the agreement.

The covenant was a solemn pact formalizing relations between the king and his vassals. Because of the king's supremacy, the treaty was not open to discussion. The vassal's only choice was to accept or reject the offer. Still, agreeing to enter a covenant relationship was the easy part. Upholding it always proved more challenging.

Covenant Responsibilities

While camped at Sinai, Moses urged Israel to accept the gracious offer of a covenant (*berit*) relationship with God as their Ruler. The Lord delivered them from Egyptian bondage and promised His continual protection if they would pledge their faithfulness to Him as King. The people agreed to God's terms but never lived up to their words. As a result, those who escaped slavery under Pharaoh perished while wandering in the wilderness. Dying in the region's wastelands was the natural consequence of forsaking their covenant with God.

After that generation passed from the scene, a new group of Israelites stood poised on the border of Canaan ready to ford the Jordan and settle in the Promised Land. Before allowing them to cross the river, Moses exhorted his countrymen to renew the covenant between God and their nation. He did not want them to repeat the mistake that led to their parents' deaths in the desert. They needed to understand that God requires more than good intentions or big talk. He demands faithfulness from His people.

Renewal is an ongoing process. The treaty God established with Israel at Sinai was not limited to those present when it was first delivered. It was a perpetual contract. The life of every Israelite was bound to God through Moses' Law until the arrival of Christ. Consequently, every generation was called upon to recommit themselves to the Lord as King. Covenant loyalty was both a national trust and a personal commitment. For individuals within Israel, honoring the covenant was a daily endeavor and a lifelong pursuit. Constancy, therefore, is fundamental to the concept of spiritual renewal, and complacency will forever remain the mortal enemy of the soul.

Covenant Love

The primary feature of the covenant was the intimate bond it established between God and His people. Covenant is about relationship, and love was the dynamic force underlying this accord. God's love led to the formation of the covenant with Israel, and only by returning His love could they participate in it. Spiritual renewal, therefore, is fundamentally a renewal of the commitment to love. The command to love did not lessen its value but revealed God's understanding of man's forgetful nature. The Lord knew humanity's need for constant encouragement.

Submission to covenant stipulations was the tangible means through which the Israelites could express their love to God. They had to be careful, however, not to allow that love to degenerate into mere legalism. Obedience must come from the heart to be acceptable. The object of every commandment was to preserve and enhance the spiritual connection between God and man. Disobedience disrupted that vital relationship.

Covenant Christianity

Faith and obedience are no less important in the gospel age than when God first established His covenant at Sinai. Like the Israelites camped on the plains of Moab, every human being stands poised on the threshold of a future that will bring either blessing or cursing. The choice is a personal one that God allows each individual to make. Who will rule as king in the heart of man? Will it be the cruel taskmaster of sin, more harsh and tyrannical than Pharaoh himself? Or will it be the heavenly Father whose love and kindness make it a joy to serve Him? The Lord is King of kings, and it is only in relationship with Him that man can rise above sin to enjoy spiritual fulfillment and abundant life.

"Conversion" is the term used to describe how a person enters a covenant relationship with God today. From the human side, the contract is initiated by faith and sealed in baptism. Jesus warned those contemplating this action to count the cost before obligating themselves (Luke 14:27-33). Breaking faith with God is a serious matter with grave consequences. A covenant is never something to be entered into lightly, but especially when that covenant is with the Lord. It is not enough to talk of commitment to Christ and His covenant. Devotion must be demonstrated in daily life. Perfection is not the issue, yet conduct reveals the authenticity of professed love for God.

Covenant Hearts

At the same time, it must be acknowledged that most attempts at renewal focus unduly on the outer, rather than inner, man. Real and lasting change must take place in the heart. From there, a person's words and actions will align themselves with the soul's internal compass. Although human effort is involved, the divine power necessary to succeed is guaranteed (Philippians 2:12-13).

In view of what God has done in the past, the terms of the covenant are reasonable. In view of what God has promised in the future, covenant loyalty is also desirable. What lies behind and before man encourage him to love and serve the Lord in the present moment!

Moses' words to Israel concerning covenant loyalty have served as a challenge to every ensuing generation. In the Christian Age, God's people are encouraged to reaffirm their commitment to the New Covenant established by Jesus (Jeremiah 31:31; Hebrews 8:13). Constant renewal was the key to Israel's success in Canaan, and it is the secret to abundant life today. Eternal rewards await those who maintain covenant faithfulness to the end (Revelation 2:10).

With these basic principles in mind, it is time for you to begin the renewal process. If you are a Christian, begin each day by purposing to honor the covenant you made with God at your conversion. If you are not a Christian, why not submit to God's terms for entering the covenant community? Over the coming weeks, the opportunity will be yours to improve your spiritual life radically. You will be amazed at the simplicity of the biblical plan to accomplish this end. An open heart and mind are all that are needed to unleash God's renewing power in your life!

DISCUSSION

1. How is the beginning of spiritual life like conception and birth?

2. How are spiritual handicaps and physical disabilities the same? Different?

3. Explain the meaning of the word "covenant."

4. Describe four basic parts of ancient vassal treaties. How does this relate to Deuteronomy?

5. What role does love play in man's covenant relationship with God?

6. Does the fact that God commands love lessen its value?

7. What is a tangible means for expressing covenant love for God?

8. How can a person keep obedience from degenerating into legalism?

9. Why is constant renewal the key to abundant life?

10. What is necessary to unleash God's renewing power in your life?

RENEWAL ACTIVITIES

1. Write your own definitions of the word "renewal" (or spiritual renewal).

2. Determine to begin your personal spiritual renewal process now. Keep a journal of your thoughts and experiences over the next 12 weeks.

3. Complete the spiritual renewal survey on the last page of this book.

2

RENEW YOUR TRUST
"Your Priceless Past"

Many people suffer from what has been called the "hamster syndrome." Day after day, these cute creatures run their little hearts out on an exercise wheel mounted in their cages. Yet for all that effort, when they step down off the wheel, they have gone nowhere. That unproductive lifestyle may be acceptable for hamsters, but not for humans. It bothers men and women when they feel they are continuously spinning their wheels. People require a sense of purpose and accomplishment for good mental and spiritual health. They long for meaning and significance.

> **Encouragement for Renewal**
>
> *If I am to enjoy spiritual renewal, I must renew my absolute trust in God.*

Millions of people think their lives are going nowhere. As a result, they suffer symptoms ranging from wistfulness to chronic depression. Hamsters, unlike mankind, do not have hang-ups about life's big issues. They are not brooding and introspective. They do not fret over fulfilling their life-mission. Their concerns are food and water, not legacy or destiny. Obviously, hamsters and humans are not much alike.

To satisfy the unique need humans have for meaning, God has provided His highest creation with something called history. Each person has a priceless past that makes existence not only bearable but also a blessing. That story reaches back beyond one's own birth to ancient accounts of God's care for His covenant people. As we take our place with the congregation of Israel and hear Moses recount the exploits of God's love, we listen closely, knowing that their story is linked with our own.

On the plains of Moab, Moses reminded the Israelites of what God had done for them during their brief history as a nation. Deuteronomy 1:6-4:43 forms the historical prologue to the covenant treaty between the King of heaven and earth and His vassals. The Lord's track record of caring for His people was flawless. As Moses reminisced about major events of the last 40 years, he was presenting indisputable evidence that God deserved His people's confidence and devotion. His message revealed three truths that give new meaning to life for those who trust in the Lord.

You Are Loved

The exodus was Exhibit A in Moses' defense of the trustworthiness of God. The nation's deliverance from Egypt was an impressive display of God's power, but more importantly, it demonstrated the depth of His love for His people (Deuteronomy 4:37). Later, the Lord carried them through the wilderness as a father carries his son (1:31). Moses often used paternal imagery to convey the Lord's genuine concern for His people.

Jesus taught His followers to think of God in the same affectionate way. Although He is the powerful supreme being of the universe, they could call Him Father (Matthew 6:9). The comparisons between the Lord and a loving parent are nearly endless. He delights in giving good gifts to His children (7:11). He anxiously awaits the return of those who have gone astray, longing to welcome them home with open arms (Luke 15:20). Every son and daughter can look forward to an incorruptible inheritance reserved in heaven (Galatians 4:6-7; 1 Peter 1:4). Indeed, Christians have a Father whose love for them can never be exhausted.

Earth's greatest display of love took place at Calvary. John records: "For God so loved the world that He gave His only begotten Son, that whoever believes in Him should not perish but have everlasting life" (John 3:16). God's love is not an abstract idea, but an undeniable fact based on real events. If the cross says anything, it says God cares.

You Have a Purpose

Through retelling their history, Moses also reminded the Israelites that they were a people with a purpose. Moses recalled, "The Lord our God spoke to us in Horeb, saying: 'You have dwelt long enough at this mountain' " (Deuteronomy 1:6). Israel could not remain at Mount Sinai forever. The time had come for them to take possession of the Promised Land. Sadly, when the critical moment arrived, they lacked the faith to obey God and thereby fulfill His plan to place them at the crossroads of civilization as a beacon of righteousness to surrounding nations. The tragedy at Kadesh Barnea put that goal on hold for 40 years until a new group of Israelites was ready to undertake what their fathers failed to do.

God's people in every age are represented as moving forward to fulfill their place in His divine plan. Christians are exhorted by Paul to "press toward the goal for the prize of the upward call of God in Christ Jesus" (Philippians 3:14). Like Israel at Kadesh Barnea, they cannot quit because of past failures. Nor, as at Horeb, can they tarry too long in enjoyable mountaintop moments with the Lord.

Too many people are in need of the Savior for His followers to indulge themselves in idleness. Peter wanted to spend more time on the Mount of Transfiguration where Jesus was glorified, but a desperate father whose son was in trouble and needed help was anxiously awaiting Jesus at the foot of the mountain (Luke 9:28-42). Paul was exhausted from his missionary travels, yet he always found strength to press on to the next town and continue his preaching. Much work needs to be done in preparation for the Lord's return (John 9:4).

Whenever people are sick, hungry, lonely or sad, the followers of Christ are constrained by the Lord's example to lay down their lives in service to those in need. Christians are driven to action by the memory of Jesus' love and the promise of His second coming. Like John the Baptist, their mission is to prepare the way of the Lord into human hearts. Striving to fulfill that purpose makes life rich and satisfying.

You Have a Future

Moses also used Israel's history to show the possibilities of the future. Some Israelites were under the mistaken impression that the previous generation had failed to enter Canaan because of unfaithfulness or weakness on the part of God. In reality, there was no deficiency on God's part. The Israelites' disobedience led to their destruction in the desert (Deuteronomy 1:26). The Lord's command to possess the land (vv. 6-8) was accompanied with the assurance of divine assistance to complete the mission. That help, however, was conditioned on their obedience.

Moses recounted how Israel disregarded God's instructions to launch the attack on Canaan from their base camp at Kadesh Barnea (Deuteronomy 1:19-46). The wanderings that resulted were a form of discipline, not a sign of powerlessness. God can and will bless those who obey Him (vv. 36-38). Because Caleb and Joshua were faithful to God and did not join the rebellion, they were allowed to enter the Promised Land and escape the fate of their contemporaries.

Although anxious to cross the Jordan, the new generation of Israelites encamped at Moab were still fearful of what they would encounter on the other side. Moses helped them to understand that the obstacles they faced were inconsequential as long as God was with them. The giants, fortified cities and large armies of Canaan were no match for a people whose God could bring them safely out of Egypt and sustain them through the desert (Deuteronomy 2:7, 36).

As they made their way toward Canaan, the Israelites were confronted by warring nations who would not let them pass in peace. When battle erupted, God delivered the powerful kings Sihon (Deuteronomy 2:26-37) and Og (3:1-11) into their hands. Some tribes received their allotment of land from these conquered territories, and the rest took heart that the Lord would do the same for them (vv. 12-22). Just as God had defeated these Amorite kings, He would defeat the kings of Canaan (v. 21). If history was any indication, the Israelites had a bright future ahead of them.

The Christian's Hope

As Christians gather around the Lord's Table, they also look back in history and receive encouragement for the future. The ultimate display of God's love and saving power was at Calvary (1 John 3:16; 4:9-10). Paul observed of God: "He who did not spare His own Son, but delivered Him up for us all, how shall He not with Him also freely give us all things?" (Romans 8:32).

God's Word is full of promises that provide His people with courage to face the difficulties of life. He will never leave nor forsake them (Hebrews 13:5). He will graciously give them strength in times of weakness (2 Corinthians 12:9). He has the power to make all things work together for good (Romans 8:28). These promises are meaningful because the Lord has proven He can be trusted to do what He says.

Of all that God has done throughout history, the empty tomb offers mankind the greatest hope for the future. It is a reminder that death has been defeated. It is proof that Jesus will raise His followers when He returns. It is God's promise that, even now, heavenly mansions are being prepared for the faithful.

An Appeal to Faithfulness

The first three chapters of Deuteronomy retrace the history of God's dealings with His chosen people. The fourth chapter makes an appeal based on what the Lord had done for them. "Now, O Israel, listen to the statutes and the judgments which I teach you to observe, that you may live, and go in and possess the land which the Lord God of your fathers is giving you" (Deuteronomy 4:1). Moses' purpose in recounting these events was to persuade Israel to trust God implicitly. God's trustworthiness inspires confidence in His love and supplies saints with strength to face the challenges of each new day.

Moses described one final event from Israel's history to reinforce his plea. At Baal Peor, many Israelite men were seduced by Moabite women and lured into idol worship (Numbers 25:1-9). When they broke faith with God, He punished them with a pestilence (v. 8; Deuteronomy 4:3). Those who held fast to the Lord survived to enjoy untold blessings (v. 4). History is God's witness that He rewards those who keep His covenant and disciplines those who defy it.

People sometimes sit through a class on Bible history like an adolescent in Algebra I. "What good is this stuff?" they ask. "What relevance could it possibly have for my life today?" The value of knowing the past is priceless because it reveals the unchanging nature of God. It says you have a heavenly Father who loves you beyond measure. It confirms that God has a wonderful purpose for your life. Most of all, it assures you of a promising future both now and throughout eternity.

Knowing these things, we can joyfully honor the covenant of One who has done so much for His people. Those who put their complete trust in God are well on their way to substantive spiritual renewal!

DISCUSSION

1. What evidence do you see of the "hamster syndrome" in today's society? In your life?

2. What would life be like without any knowledge of the past?

3. What is the best part of having God as your Father?

4. What is your sense of God's purpose for your life?

5. How does the past help you face the future?

6. Why would God not allow Israel to remain with Him forever at Sinai?

7. Why must Christians move on from their mountaintop moments? Give examples.

8. After the events at Kadesh Barnea, how did pressing on help Israel cope with their disappointment?

9. How does the Lord's Supper evoke memories that inspire loyalty to God?

10. How is absolute trust in God linked to spiritual renewal?

RENEWAL ACTIVITIES

1. The Lord's reliability, which has been demonstrated throughout history, is inseparable from spiritual renewal. Using the letters in the word "trust," make an acrostic that describes God's faithfulness.

2. Thank God for all He has done to foster faith in His people, and ask for His help in becoming more trusting.

3

RENEW YOUR VALUES
"Ten Timeless Truths"

Parents understand the importance of rules. A home can become chaotic when everyone does just as he pleases. It also creates an unfair burden on the domestic engineer called "Mom." Periodically, parents sit down and discuss changes that need to be made for their home to run happily and for their children to mature responsibly. From these discussions comes a set of rules for all to follow.

From the parents' standpoint, these rules border on divine omniscience. Unfortunately, the children do not always share this enlightened viewpoint. Somehow, they are convinced that picking up dirty clothes and having to brush their teeth are part of a plot to undermine the enjoyment of adolescence. Those who are part of this conspiracy wonder why it is not obvious to the resistance movement that these rules are motivated by love and a sincere desire for them to enjoy a healthy, happy life. It seems that the only way to make a genuine convert is for a child to grow up and join the ranks of parents.

This scenario parallels the predicament of Israel following the ex-

> **Encouragement for Renewal**
>
> *If I am to enjoy spiritual renewal, I must renew my core values.*

odus. God gave the Israelites a set of rules at Sinai that they considered too limiting. Although they promised to do what He asked, their rebelliousness exposed their true feelings. If only they could understand that these commands were designed not to restrict happiness but to provide fullness of life.

This is where faith comes in. God asks man to trust that His desire for obedience is not an arbitrary display of omnipotence. Neither God nor good parents flex their muscles just to impress or bully their offspring. His only concern was "that it might be well with them and with their children forever" (Deuteronomy 5:29).

Heaven's love was packed into each commandment that formed the foundation of Israel's covenant relationship with God. Before delivering the Ten Commandments to a second generation of Israelites, Moses tried to communicate this principle to them. If they would listen to God and do what He instructed, they would prosper in the new land they were about to enter (Deuteronomy 4:1). God's words were neither optional nor negotiable (v. 2). If that sounds unfair, it is only so to those who do not know God. Because He is love (1 John 4:8), that divine characteristic permeated His law.

Moses told the Israelites that by keeping the righteous ordinances of the law, their religious neighbors would stand in awe of their wisdom and discernment (Deuteronomy 4:6). Jesus said the same thing when He referred to His followers as "the light of the world" (Matthew 5:14-16). When men behold the integrity and joy of genuine Christian living, the natural result is to glorify the Father in heaven from whom it derives. Real greatness for nations or individuals is not wealth or power but a lifestyle of righteousness that evidences a living relationship with God. Such a life is possible only through keeping the covenant.

The Ten Commandments clearly defined the relationship between God and the Israelites. It summarized their responsibilities as His subjects. These covenant duties and obligations formed the core of the vassal treaty between the Lord and His people, and the principles underlying these laws are vitally important even today.

Deuteronomy 4:44-5:5 introduces the Ten Commandments. In these verses, Moses was careful to identify himself as the mediator, rather than the originator of these transcendent truths (5:4-5, 22-23). His job was to urge the people to heed God's commands (v. 1).

The foundation of covenant fellowship is a dynamic combination of law and love. Unfortunately, some view law as the antithesis of love. Legal requirements associated with adoption or marriage do not lessen the love of a parent or spouse. To the contrary, they are high expressions of devotion and commitment.

The Bible frequently compares the relationship between God and man to marriage. A man who tells a woman he loves her and wants to live with her but is unwilling to comply with legal requirements to become her husband denies his words by his actions. Those who claim to love God yet refuse to keep His Word are no different.

Moses put the commandments in their proper context by identifying the Lord as the one who delivered Israel from bondage in Egypt (Deuteronomy 5:6). The commandments were legitimate expectations in view of what God had done for them. The God of the exodus deserved the loyalty of those He had liberated. In the new land, Israel would be tempted to acquire new gods, but for their sake, it was a temptation they must resist.

Man's Relationship With God

The first four commands dealt with man's relationship to God.

• "You shall have no other gods before Me" (Deuteronomy 5:7). The Lord began by demanding absolute faithfulness from Israel to whom He had already proven His faithfulness. Every aspect of life should be dominated by exclusive loyalty to God. Anything that relegates God to second place in a person's priorities can be considered a violation of this first commandment. That is why the New Testament refers to covetousness as a form of idolatry (Colossians 3:5). The God of the covenant must be the controlling force in all of life. Every move away from God is a mistake regardless of the distance or direction.

God promised to guard jealously His preeminent place in the hearts of His people. Unlike human jealousy, God's motives were untainted by selfishness. Everything He did was based on His intense love for man. The Lord was genuinely concerned with Israel's welfare, and He knew their only hope for abundant life was maintaining unbroken fellowship with Him.

• "You shall not make for yourself a carved image" (Deuteronomy 5:8). Any attempt to represent the transcendent God in forms like those of Canaanite or Egyptian idols was prohibited (4:16-19). God's being invisible was significant because His invisibility related to His transcendence. Any form proved inadequate because it imposed a limit on the Infinite One.

Moses warned that disregarding this directive would have far reaching consequences. Children could suffer for many generations if parents failed to impart an understanding of God's distinctive spirit nature. Those who bowed down before representations of God modeled after the created order soon forgot the Lord. In contrast, those who kept this command were continual beneficiaries of His loving kindness.

• "You shall not take the name of the Lord your God in vain" (Deuteronomy 5:11). Israel's welfare was also connected with respecting the name of God. People of that age commonly believed that the names of deities possessed implicit power. They were considered magical charms that could be used to control the gods and harness their supernatural gifts. Using the Lord's name as an incantation was an affront to His sovereignty.

In modern times, it is not unusual to hear the name of God tossed around casually in conversation. This practice desensitizes people to the awesome majesty of the God of the covenant. Christians should be careful to speak God's name in a way that communicates its sacredness and His greatness. Its casual use is not for getting laughs or acquiring personal gain. It is not for increasing the force of a curse or promise. It is not to be muttered mindlessly in songs and prayers without due thought and reverence. These inappropriate acts dishonor the name that is above every name and injure the one who invokes it in such a disrespectful manner.

• "Observe the Sabbath day, to keep it holy" (Deuteronomy 5:12). The Lord commanded the Israelites to observe the Sabbath as a day of rest and spiritual renewal. Sanctifying the seventh day was a distinctive characteristic of the covenant. It reflected an understanding of dependence upon the powerful God of creation, who completed His work in six days. The Sabbath marked the day God ceased His creative activity and foreshadowed the greater rest of heaven that awaits the faithful.

Although the work ban is no longer in force, there are many similarities between the Sabbath and Sunday, the Lord's Day of the new covenant (Revelation 1:10). The Sabbath was linked to the creation of a new nation. Sunday is linked to individuals becoming a new creation in Christ Jesus (2 Corinthians 5:17). The Lord understood the importance of setting aside a time when families could renew their relationship with Him through worship and study.

A high view of God was essential for personal holiness. Respect was to be paid to God's supreme status, spirit nature, sacred name and special day. The intent behind each of these instructions was to guard against any disruption of the loving relationship between God and His people. It also formed the basis of man's relationship to his fellowman made in God's image. If a person did not show respect for God, how much less would he consider the rights and needs of other people.

Man's Relationship With Man

The last six commands describe how the Israelites were to relate to one another as an outgrowth of a proper relationship with God.

• "Honor your father and your mother" (Deuteronomy 5:16). Family will always be at the core of the covenant. The home is God's training ground for practicing its precepts. The parent-child relationship should prepare a person to relate appropriately with God and with authority figures one must deal with throughout life. When a child honors and obeys his parents, he is developing the relational skills needed for effectively interacting with others. Honoring father and mother also provides an atmosphere in the home favorable for imparting covenant beliefs to the next generation.

Submitting to parental authority is a challenging faith issue for many adolescents. Limited life experience makes it hard to understand why parents make certain demands or impose certain restrictions. God asks young people to demonstrate their trust in Him by submitting to their mothers and fathers. By doing so, children express faith and love that will not go unrewarded. The promise accompanying this command suggests that God knew how difficult it could be.

• "You shall not murder" (Deuteronomy 5:17). The sixth commandment was an unmistakable affirmation of the sacredness of human life. The Hebrew term here should not be misunderstood as for-bidding capital punishment or self-defense. It prohibits taking life for personal reasons as in murder.

Man was not to become judge, jury and executioner for those who offended or inconvenienced him. Life, whether born or unborn, came under divine protection through the covenant. This provision was traced to the inherent worth of all human life as a result of its cre-ation in God's image (Genesis 9:6).

Destructive emotions are also prohibited by this command. Feelings such as hatred and jealously are precursors to murder (1 John 3:15). Animosity damages relationships and creates an atmosphere conducive to cruelty and violence. Renewal occurs whenever negative, dehu-manizing thoughts are rejected and compassionate, life-affirming atti-tudes are embraced.

• "You shall not commit adultery" (Deuteronomy 5:18). The seventh commandment prohibited sexual relations between two individuals not married to each other. The Lord intended sex to be enjoyed in the con-text of trust and commitment within the marriage bond. God's desire for faithfulness in marriage is the same as in His own covenant with man. Intimate relationships are based on loyalty between husband and wife. Over time, that devotion produces a comforting sense of securi-ty. When trust is betrayed, relationships can disintegrate rapidly.

This commandment is especially important in today's sex-saturated society. Maintaining moral purity in light of Satan's all-out effort to un-dermine the foundation of healthy families requires real faith. Those who choose to break faith with their spouses are simultaneously break-ing faith with God. Those who maintain covenant faithfulness with their spouses will enjoy special blessings that are the natural consequence of fidelity. Peace of mind, mutual respect, affection and trust are among the benefits reserved for those who honor their marriage vows.

• "You shall not steal" (Deuteronomy 5:19). This command was set in terms of the worst possible kind of theft: kidnapping. Joseph's experi-ence of being sold into slavery by his brothers was a violation of this law. In principle, what applies to people also pertains to property. Taking what belongs to another person is wrong in any situation, whether health, life, freedom, reputation or personal effects. The people of God should regard their fellowman and his belongings as sacred.

Stealing exhibits a selfish mind-set with little regard for others. The remedy is for a thief to imagine himself in the position of his victim (Matthew 7:12). Empathy has the power to alter one's outlook and course of action. Therefore, renewal is a byproduct of ever-increasing concern for the well-being of others. Such an attitude makes robbery unthinkable and generosity irresistible (Ephesians 4:28).

• "You shall not bear false witness" (Deuteronomy 5:20). The context of this command was Israel's legal system. The Lord knew that some would be tempted to corrupt justice through false testimony to advance their personal interests. Although Moses specifically forbade dishonesty in court dealings, the principle underlying this directive demanded a rejection of deception in all of its various forms. It is impossible to have a meaningful relationship apart from truthful communication. Just as God had been completely honest with His people, He expected them to be forthright with one another. In principle, God was calling for honesty as the standard for all human discourse.

• "You shall not covet your neighbor's wife" (Deuteronomy 5:21). The final tenet of the Ten Commandments focused on the incentive to do wrong rather than a particular act of disobedience. The concern was "why" rather than "what." Thus, the 10th commandment summarized the message of this entire section.

To covet is to desire something (or someone) very strongly. Its use in this passage suggests an improper kind of desire rooted in consuming self-interest. Most problems are the result of selfishness dominating a person's thinking and actions. Only by controlling desire can behavior be controlled. This requires putting God and others before personal interests. When life is directed by this rule, it produces stability in society, harmony in the home, and peace within one's own heart.

Principle-Centered Living

The Law of Moses is no longer the covenant of God's people (Jeremiah 31:31; Hebrews 8:6-13). Still, there is no less need for exclusive loyalty to God and heartfelt obedience to His Word. Christians seeking spiritual renewal are sometimes limited to a vague, emotional experience. Real renewal cannot be divorced from keeping God's commands.

Christian living is principle-centered living. The principles guiding the life of Jesus are revealed in the New Testament and should be adopted by His followers. Abundant life awaits those who, by faith, are continually of the mind to fear God and keep His commandments. Spiritual renewal is underway when people determine to make their words and deeds an outgrowth of heavenly values rather than of earthly impulses.

DISCUSSION

1. Name the Ten Commandments.

2. How can these commandments be broken down into two groups?

3. Why is God's demand for preeminence not a sign of selfishness?

4. What is significant about respecting the invisibility of God?

5. In what ways might a person use God's name vainly?

6. How is Sunday like the Sabbath? How is it different? Suggest some ways it can be used for spiritual renewal today.

7. What is the connection between the first four commandments and those that follow?

8. Why do you think the command to honor one's parents comes first among God's laws concerning man's relationship to man?

9. Why can spiritual renewal never be divorced from keeping God's commands?

10. Using the word "respect," summarize each of the commandments.

RENEWAL ACTIVITIES

1. Working individually or in small groups, summarize the Ten Commandments in a single sentence.

2. If God commissioned you to write an 11th commandment, what would it be?

3. If God allowed mankind to amend or repeal one of the Ten Commandments, which one do you think most people would choose?

4

RENEW YOUR COMMITMENT
"Wholeheartedness"

Many Americans have adopted the philosophy that it makes little difference which religion a person chooses to follow. Attend the church, mosque or synagogue of your choice. It does not matter what you believe so long as you believe it sincerely. Tolerance and broadmindedness are the only "sacred" teachings that must never be compromised. The most grievous of all errors is to promote any kind of religious exclusivity.

Moses would be considered narrow-minded by today's pluralistic standards. His "outlandish" belief in one God would offend millions of people with loyalties to different deities and religions. It probably had a similar effect upon the Egyptians, Canaanites and Mesopotamians when he first spoke these words more than 3,000 years ago. "Just who do you think you are, Moses? What makes you think that the Lord is the only God? Believe in the Lord if you want, but how about a little respect for Amon-Re, Baal and Marduk?"

How would Moses respond to such criticisms? Would he apologize

---

Encouragement for Renewal

If I am to enjoy spiritual renewal, I must renew the wholeness of my love for God.

and chart a more politically correct course. No! Moses was a prophet, not a corrupt politician. Rather than change his convictions, he would attempt to change his opponents' minds by presenting the evidence in support of his claim.

Standing With Moses

Christians should stand with Moses in his covenant conviction that the Lord alone is God. Yet even those who claim to believe this truth are not affected in the same way. Intellectual acknowledgement can sometimes become an end in itself. James declared, "You believe that there is one God. You do well. Even the demons believe – and tremble! But do you want to know, O foolish man, that faith without works is dead?" (James 2:19-20). Those who profess belief in one God but do not order their lives by His will have a demonic kind of faith. James declared that faith must express itself in daily conduct if it is to be beneficial. Belief that does not change a person's behavior is worthless.

Some people are afraid of what others will think if they become serious about their faith. If they radically reorient their lives according to the teachings of Christ, they might be labeled "fanatics." If they show enthusiasm and devotion in athletics, education or business, people admire their accomplishments. Show the same dedication in running the Christian race, and the response is often different. Christians excel in many fields of endeavor, but the energy they invest to evangelize, grow in virtue or serve others is not always understood or appreciated.

Peter warned that the unconverted would often think it strange when Christians do not behave in the same worldly ways they do (1 Peter 4:4). All that some people understand is power, pleasure and profit. What is a Christian to do? Too frequently, the response is to live in two worlds. Behavior on Sunday becomes conspicuously different from behavior the rest of the week. This attempt to compartmentalize life is a recipe for physical, emotional and spiritual disaster. Moses wanted the Israelites to know that people who choose this course are fooling no one but themselves. God does not accept half-hearted devotion. He wants man's all or nothing. Wholeheartedness is a prerequisite to spiritual renewal and a satisfying relationship with God.

The Shema

Deuteronomy 6:1-3 is an introduction to the central and greatest commandment in all of Scripture. Moses pointed out three things before proceeding. First, the object of all that God commanded was to cause man to "fear" Him. This term described the respectful but affectionate demeanor of a vassal before his king or a son before his father. The proof of such a reverent attitude was obedience, and the end result was long life. These verses capsulized the aims, expectations and benefits of the covenant to encourage compliance with its decrees.

The next two verses form the most fundamental teaching in all of God's Word. The rest of Deuteronomy and the entire Bible merely elaborate on the principles presented here. "Hear, O Israel: The Lord our God, the Lord is one! You shall love the Lord your God with all your heart, with all your soul, and with all your strength" (6:4-5). These words make up what is commonly known as the "Shema," a Hebrew word meaning "hear." It is still recited on a daily basis by many devout Jews. The command to hear was a challenge to give serious consideration to what would follow.

After getting the people's attention, Moses presented Israel with two of the covenant's most foundational concepts. One pertained to the nature of God. The other concerned man's proper response to God in view of His special nature.

One Lord

"The Lord our God, the Lord is one!" This simple statement rocked the pagan world. Monotheism, belief in and commitment to one God, was a revolutionary idea to most ancient people. God's oneness is a concept that conveys two important ideas – God's unity and uniqueness. Christians are aware that God exists in three persons, sometimes referred to as the "Trinity." This does not mean that there are three Gods, but that the Father, Son and Spirit exist together as the one true God. Hints of this unity may be found from the opening chapter of the Bible where it declares, "Let Us make man in Our image, according to Our likeness" (Genesis 1:26).

The oneness of a husband and wife is patterned after the special relationship between members of the Godhead. It is a paradigm for the organization of local churches where men of equality take on functional differences and work together in complete harmony. The unity of God's divine essence and holy purpose overshadow His diversity.

Even greater emphasis can be laid upon God's uniqueness. The Lord is not merely one God among many. He is not even first among the greatest. He is the one and only God! There is no other like Him because there is no other.

One Response

Growing out of this elemental truth is man's primary duty to love God above all else. Obedience is essential to the fulfillment of this charge. Jesus confirmed the indispensable link between love and obedience when He urged, "If you love Me, keep My commandments" (John 14:15). Obedience must always be regulated by a loving relationship with God. Anything less is merely legalism. The obedience that God wants must be cheerful and voluntary. As John explained, "For this is the love of God, that we keep His commandments. And His commandments are not burdensome" (1 John 5:3).

Notice that the word "all" is used to describe the kind of love God wants (Deuteronomy 6:5). Spiritual renewal is the process of learning to love God more completely. There can be no holding back of the heart. This all-encompassing love may be compared to the exclusivity of intimacy within the marriage bond. If a husband reserves his romantic love for his wife "most" of the time, should she be pleased? If he gives her 90 percent of his devotion, is that enough? The term that best describes such partial loyalty is "adultery." God is no less offended when man offers Him fragments of faithfulness.

Love's Dimensions

Loving God with "all your heart, with all your soul, and with all your strength" implies many dimensions to one's spiritual renewal.

• *Heart.* When Moses proclaimed this grand commandment, he enlisted every human faculty in the delightful duty of loving the One Who first loved him. He began with the heart as the center of man's mind, will and emotions. A rational (mind), determined (will) and affectionate (emotions) love is a necessary part of the proper response to the precedent of God's own redeeming love.

Mind. The Lord wants more than blind sentimentality. He wants the love of faith that comes from human intellect persuaded by reason and revelation that He exists and rewards those who diligently seek Him (Hebrews 11:6). Love is on display whenever someone searches the Scriptures to know God and His perfect will.

Will. The Lord wants more than fair-weather faith. He wants a devotion that thrives in both good times and bad. Momentary love that comes and goes with a person's moods is coincidence rather than devotion (1 Corinthians 15:58).

Emotions. The Lord wants more than legalism. Cold, unemotional, detached obedience is unappealing to God or man. Callous compliance is the complete opposite of the warm and tender connection that should exist between the Lord and His covenant people.

• *Soul.* Moses' second petition was to love God with all of the soul. Perhaps the terms "heart," "soul" and "strength" were used almost interchangeably to emphasize the entirety of devotion sought by the Father. However, the meanings appear to be more specialized than that.

"Soul" may have been used to indicate that the love God seeks must involve man's very life or being. It is expressed in the motto "to live is Christ" (Philippians 1:21). This was the kind of love implied by Paul when he said, "I have been crucified with Christ; it is no longer I who live, but Christ lives in me" (Galatians 2:20). Ideally, when a person's covenant relationship with God is what it should be, a state is reached in which living is synonymous with loving God.

• *Strength.* To love God with all of one's strength suggests the employment of human strength in service to the one true God. No love is complete that does not spend itself in labor on behalf of the one loved. This rule holds true in marriage, parenting, friendship and every other relationship. How much more should energy and effort be expended to honor the Lord? Paul wrote, "For in Christ Jesus neither circumcision nor uncircumcision avails anything, but faith working through love" (Galatians 5:6).

Wholeheartedness

Near the end of his life, Joshua noticed that idolatry was increasing among the Israelites. They worshiped the Lord but paid homage to numerous Canaanite deities as well. Joshua scolded the people: "choose for yourselves this day whom you will serve" (Joshua 24:15). They could honor the Lord or Baal, but not both. Years later, Elijah asked the idolatrous Israelites of his day, "How long will you falter between two opinions? If the Lord is God, follow Him" (1 Kings 18:21). The pleas of Elijah and Joshua grew out of Moses' declaration that there was only one true God and that He deserved absolute allegiance.

Joshua and Caleb are prime examples of the kind of devotion pleasing to God. When Israel rebelled at Kadesh Barnea, the Lord announced that He would not allow those who were 20 and older to enter the Promised Land. An exception was made for Joshua and Caleb because they followed the Lord (Deuteronomy 1:36-38). That same kind of dedicated love will bring God's blessings today.

In the Shema, Moses underscores the quality of love God desires from His covenant people – a wholehearted, committed kind of love that affects every dimension of a person's life. Renewal is possible only to the extent that love for God is complete and entire. An undivided heart is the essence of spiritual renewal. Love for God must be untainted and unrestricted. In the words of Jesus, "Blessed are the pure in heart, For they shall see God" (Matthew 5:8).

DISCUSSION

1. In today's pluralistic world, is it narrow-minded to believe in one God exclusively? Explain.

2. How should belief in one God demonstrate itself in a person's life?

3. Why are people afraid of what others will think if they devote their lives completely to the Lord?

4. How can the Bible be seen as a commentary on the command to love God wholeheartedly?

5. What does it mean to love God with all your heart?

6. How can a person love God with all his or her soul?

7. What does it mean to love God with all your might?

8. What are some symptoms of half-hearted Christianity?

9. What is the greatest hindrance to wholehearted Christianity?

10. Why does renewal occur in proportion to the completeness of a person's love for God?

RENEWAL ACTIVITIES

1. Beginning now, purpose that you will love God without any reservations.

2. Working privately, ask yourself how your love for God has not been as complete as you think it should be. Make a list of changes you would like to make to integrate your faith into your daily life.

5

RENEW YOUR FAMILY
"How to Impress Your Children"

To live happy and successful lives, children need a good set of values. It would be nice if babies came preprogrammed with heavenly standards, but morals must be taught over many years to become part of their personalities. That is why the covenant is central to becoming good parents and building good character in children.

At one time in this country, parents, churches and schools worked together closely to impart virtuous life principles to the next generation. Where are today's children learning their values? For many adolescents, this important job is being done by celebrities and peers. America's youth are patterning their lives after recording artists, movie actors and professional athletes.

> **Encouragement for Renewal**
>
> *If I am to enjoy spiritual renewal, I must renew my devotion to my family.*

Solomon advised against asking why the old days were better than these (Ecclesiastes 7:10). Instead of dreaming about the past, God's people must look to the future. Instead of glorifying days gone by, they must take advantage of the present. Sitting around complaining about the difficulties of raising children in a postmodern society does nothing to change or improve the situation.

Parents need to intensify their efforts to create values in their children. This process is one of the most vital aspects of spiritual renewal. To view religious devotion as a purely individual matter is a mistake. Commitment to the covenant seldom occurs in isolation. It is an intergenerational endeavor involving parents, grandparents and children. The family is God's most basic tool to encourage a healthy relationship with Him. That was Moses' point when he declared:

> Hear, O Israel: The Lord our God, the Lord is one! You shall love the Lord your God with all your heart, with all your soul, and with all your strength. And these words which I command you today shall be in your heart. You shall teach them diligently to your children, and shall talk of them when you sit in your house, when you walk by the way, when you lie down, and when you rise up (Deuteronomy 6:4-7).

Instruction

According to Moses, we have two two chief ways to impart values to children. The first is through teaching. According to Moses, this is primarily a function of parents. The community may assist in the process, but parents are the key players. The home – not high school or Hollywood – is where life's most important lessons should be learned. Success in this endeavor will require serious changes for many families.

In the final verse of the Old Testament, Malachi predicted the coming of John the Baptist who would turn the "hearts of the fathers to the children, And the heart of the children to their fathers" (4:6; Luke 1:17). Today's parents also need to turn their attention from the world to the needs of their sons and daughters. Materialism and the pursuit of pleasure steal away limited time and energy resources that should be devoted to the family. Rugged determination is required to stand against the tide of misplaced priorities to put the home first.

Women are often more attentive to the spiritual development of children, but God wants fathers to know that, as head of their families, He will hold them accountable first and foremost. Paul taught, "[F]athers, do not provoke your children to wrath, but bring them up in the training and admonition of the Lord" (Ephesians 6:4). Ideally, both parents should work together to instill a value system that will last a lifetime. When parents speak with one voice, the power of their message is greatly multiplied. Jesus warned, "Every kingdom divided against itself is brought to desolation, and every city or house divided against itself will not stand" (Matthew 12:25). These words are especially true when it comes to rearing a family.

"Diligent" is a good word to describe the kind of effort necessary to be effective parents today (Deuteronomy 6:7). Moses said good parenting is a task that begins when you get up in the morning and continues until you go to sleep at night. This level of devotion is essential if the Lord's commands are to permeate every sphere of a child's life. It will require a conscious and constant effort to pass on Christian values. Intent and initiative are fundamental to God's idea of parenting.

Church attendance cannot take the place of Bible instruction in the home. Rather, it is God's support system to undergird the teaching of parents. Ideally, the values taught by mothers and fathers are reinforced by teachers and youth ministers. As Solomon said, "[A] threefold cord is not quickly broken" (Ecclesiastes 4:12). When the home, school and church unite in their efforts to impart good values to the next generation, it is much more difficult for Satan to undermine their commitment to God.

Imitation

A second way of creating values in children is by example. Moses encouraged modeling as an effective means of parenting when he said, "And these words which I command you today shall be in your heart" (Deuteronomy 6:6). How will God's words be imbedded in the heart of a son or daughter if they are not first rooted in the heart of a mom and dad? The old saying, "A stream never rises higher than its source," is an appropriate proverb for parenting. Nothing provokes a child to wrath more quickly than hearing a parent say one thing and doing another. In fact, the best predictor of delinquency among youth is the disparity of their parents' words and actions.

In addition to creating values through teaching and modeling, parents should strive to limit their child's exposure to negative influences that can erode faith and undermine morality during the critical formative years. What children see and hear has a subtle but cumulative effect on their value formation. There is no question that movies, music videos and magazines affect the thinking and behavior of consumers, especially during childhood and adolescence. Particularly frightening is to imagine what young people are introduced to on the Internet while waiting for Mom and Dad to get home from work each afternoon.

Paul said Christians should focus their thoughts on things that are wholesome and holy (Philippians 4:8). In fact, Paul taught that the goal should be to bring every thought into captivity to Christ (2 Corinthians 10:4-5). That means a firm but fair policy concerning entertainment is necessary for instilling good values in children. As children grow older, parents should help them develop their own ability to select movies and music appropriate for Christian consumption.

It is also possible to exercise some control over the influence of a child's peers. Parents are often deceived into thinking that, if they train their children well, it makes no difference with whom they spend time. Paul warned that evil companions corrupt good morals (1 Corinthians 15:33). Worldly friends have a corrupting influence that breaks down the moral resolve of the best-behaved young people. Other parents have convinced themselves that they have no control over their child's choice of associates. This may be a sincerely misguided belief or a simple cop-out, but in either case, it is wrong.

Granted, when children reach adolescence, they move away from their parents toward their peers. At that point, parental opinions may seem about as important to teens as U.S. foreign policy. It is difficult, yet not impossible, to discourage unhealthy relationships after they have been established. How much better, though, to develop the right kind of friendships in the first place.

An early start helps keep children involved in an active youth group. Spending time with strong Christian families who have children of similar ages provides natural opportunities to create healthy relationships. Christian colleges and campus ministries offer college-age young people the kind of atmosphere that will encourage right choices in their lives.

The word for "teach" in Deuteronomy 6:7 means parents are to write, engrave or impress the commandments of God upon the hearts of their offspring. Parents can impress their children by teaching and modeling God's will for their lives. In this age of technological innovation, these two essentials have not changed. Values should be derived from a study of God's Word and imparted to children with resolve. Every child should be impressed with the teachings of the New Testament and taught to love God with a whole heart.

Spiritual renewal is a family affair that requires putting children ahead of career advancement and personal pleasure. Building a strong Christian home is a fun and rewarding way to renew your relationship with God. Is it time you turned your heart back to your family?

DISCUSSION

1. Name some celebrities from whom children are getting their values today.

2. Share your ideas for teaching Christian values in the home.

3. How important is diligence in raising children?

4. Do parents have the right to supervise what their children are exposed to in the media?

5. How do evil companions corrupt good morals?

6. How important is it for young people to be involved in a youth group?

7. What is the greatest hindrance to parenting today?

8. How can parents influence older children in a positive way?

9. Name a value you would like to impart to your child.

10. Explain how spiritual renewal is directly tied to family life.

RENEWAL ACTIVITIES

1. What are the major causes of parental distraction today?

2. Have different men lead the class in prayer asking for God's help in producing spiritual renewal through greater devotion to the family.

6

RENEW YOUR GRATITUDE
"Spiritual Alzheimer's"

Alzheimer's disease is a brain disorder characterized by loss of memory. In the early stages, victims try to conceal their forgetfulness by writing notes to themselves in order to recall names and other details. As the illness progresses, the memory grows worse and is manifested in poor judgment and increasingly irrational behavior.

The counterpart of this physical disease is a sickness of the soul called spiritual Alzheimer's. Christians suffering from this malady also experience loss of memory. At first, they lose sight of God's past blessings, and then they forget their present dependence upon Him. Poor judgment follows forgetfulness, and unchristian behavior is not far behind. Eventually there is a breakdown of all meaningful spiritual life.

> ◆
>
> **Encouragement for Renewal**
>
> *If I am to enjoy spiritual renewal, I must renew my sense of gratitude.*

Diagnosis

This disease is by no means new. Moses first diagnosed the condition more than 3,000 years ago. On the plains of Moab, he warned the

Israelites about the high risk of contracting such an illness in the new land they were about to enter. He knew that prosperity makes one particularly susceptible to spiritual Alzheimer's. Affluence leads to pride, pride to ingratitude, and ingratitude to spiritual death. When God is forgotten, no hope remains for man.

With spiritual Alzheimer's, forgetfulness is much more than absentmindedness. Biblical facts may be remembered, but their significance becomes blurred until God ceases to be a real presence and governing force in life. The human ego takes center stage as if mere wit and strength were the key to all of man's accomplishments (Deuteronomy 8:17). Forgotten is the God of heaven who gives life and health and opportunity to each as He pleases (v. 18).

Prognosis

Moses feared the effects of prosperity upon Israel once they entered Canaan. He understood that God's blessings could easily become a curse if taken for granted. Affluence is not inherently evil, but many temptations are associated with it. The real issue is a person's attitude, or more precisely, gratitude.

Soon the Israelites would build fine houses and settle down in the new land. They would eat to their fill and be satisfied with the bountiful harvests of Canaan. Their flocks would grow large, their wealth would increase, and all they had would be multiplied. Moses pleaded for them not to let their hearts grow proud and cause them to forget the Lord (Deuteronomy 8:11, 14). How sad to accept all these gifts and forget the One who gave them!

Immunization

When God liberated Israel from Egypt, He used the wilderness to humble and test His people before allowing them to enter the Promised Land. This was a kind of inoculation against spiritual Alzheimer's. The wilderness experiences of life remove all worldly props and cast one back on God who alone can sustain man. In the dreadful desert, Israel was made fully aware that God is the true source of life. His words are more basic to man's existence than food itself (Deuteronomy 8:3).

The wilderness makes or breaks a man, but its severity is not without a purpose. God disciplines those He loves as a father disciplines his son (Deuteronomy 8:5). Through life's difficulties, God teaches His children to remember His presence. The lesson to be learned is not self-sufficiency but the all sufficiency of God in whom they should put their trust.

Heartache and hard times are not signs that God does not exist or that a person is unloved. God allows man's wilderness moments to humble and test him so that, in the end, it will go well with him (Deuteronomy 8:16). People can easily forget God until a time of extremity shatters their self-confidence and reminds them again of the One who is their strength (2 Corinthians 12:7-9). However painful times in the wilderness may be, they are prompted by love and profitable in the end if met with faith (Hebrews 12:11-12; James 1:2-5).

More Preventive Care

Like Israel, Americans also live in a good land. God has blessed citizens of the United States with a prosperous nation in which to live. We eat and are satisfied, live in comfortable housing, and enjoy a standard of living that is the envy of the world. No generation on earth has ever been more susceptible to spiritual Alzheimer's. God does not want Americans to feel guilty about their affluence. He simply asks them not to forget Him. His gifts must not become more important than their Giver!

Spiritual Values

The appalling pride often accompanying prosperity must be resisted. What can Christians do to protect themselves against this epidemic of materialism? First, they must remember what is of true value. Jesus quoted Moses' words to clarify what is really important in life: "It is written, 'Man shall not live by bread alone, but by every word that proceeds out of the mouth of God' " (Matthew 4:4). Just as the body needs to be fed, clothed and housed, so does the soul. God's Word will nourish it (1 Peter 2:2); it may be clothed with Christ (Galatians 3:26-27); and housed in heaven after this life (John 14:1-3; 2 Corinthians 5:1). For optimal spiritual health, Christians must learn once and for all that life does not consist in the abundance of things a man possesses (Luke 12:15).

Thankful Hearts

Another step in the prevention of spiritual Alzheimer's is to remember continually God's past blessings. For Israel, that meant reflecting on God's graciousness as experienced in the exodus and desert wanderings (Deuteronomy 8:2-4). For Christians, it means centering their minds on the love God displayed when He gave His only begotten Son for the sins of the world. When Jesus instituted the Lord's Supper, He said, "[D]o this in remembrance of Me" (1 Corinthians 11:24-25). Each week (Acts 20:7) as Christians gather around the Lord's Table, they put away worldly thoughts to remember the Giver of every good and perfect gift (James 1:17) and the greatest gift He ever gave (2 Corinthians 9:15).

Paul taught the Thessalonians to give thanks in everything (1 Thessalonians 5:18). This begins with cultivating a consciousness of what is truly important or blessed in life. The natural response is to express appreciation for the source of such joyous blessings.

There is no situation in life in which a thoughtful Christian cannot find reason to express thanksgiving to God. Behind each moment and each care, the spiritually discerning eye can see the presence and provision of the Father in heaven. Even in the midst of misfortune, there is ample opportunity for praising the Lord.

Christians are not necessarily thankful for adversity, but they are to be thankful in it (Romans 8:28). For instance, they can be thankful that they do not face trials alone. God has promised to be with His people and provide the power necessary for them to overcome hardship and discouragement. Unpleasant as they may be, trying circumstances can make a person stronger in the end. They also provide a means of testing and proving love for God. Genuine gratitude is demonstrated in covenant faithfulness through obedience to God's commands.

Moments of Reflection

A good memory is a sign of good health. Forgetfulness, on the other hand, is a symptom of declining fitness. This is true spiritually as well as physically. Moses understood that the key to spiritual renewal was man's memory and that the essence of forgetfulness was disobedience. The Israelites' preoccupation with earthly prosperity caused them to neglect the Lord, and their inattentiveness to the covenant resulted in death and exile (Deuteronomy 8:20).

By calling to mind the goodness of God, man's gratitude motivates him to serve the Lord faithfully. That is why daily Bible reading and prayer are vital to spiritual health. They are touchstones with heaven and what is truly meaningful in life. It is also why ordinary cares of daily life are one of the biggest threats to spiritual renewal (Luke 8:14). Constant demands and deadlines crowd God into the background until, for all practical purposes, He is forgotten. Covenant faithfulness is the result of seeking first the kingdom of God.

Having a good relationship with God is not possible while taking Him for granted. For this reason, the Lord commands, "Be still, and know that I am God" (Psalm 46:10). Appreciation demonstrates man's recognition of his own limitations and God's infinite power and love. Thanklessness is a declaration of independence that constitutes the worst kind of idolatry: self-worship. Developing a heart of gratitude is an essential part of reviving your spiritual life.

DISCUSSION

1. Is prosperity a blessing or a curse? Explain your answer.

2. Do you think God still uses difficult life experiences to test His people as He did in the wilderness? Give some examples.

3. Why is it difficult to have prosperity and humility at the same time? Whom do you know that has achieved this elusive goal?

4. What did Moses mean when he spoke about "forgetting" God?

5. What did Moses mean when he spoke about "remembering" God?

6. What is the relationship between gratitude and obedience?

7. How does living in America today compare with the temptations faced by Israel in Canaan?

8. How did God use Israel's wilderness experiences to prepare them for prosperity in Canaan? How can adversity be spiritually renewing?

9. How prevalent is the problem of spiritual Alzheimer's in the church today?

10. Discuss the association between spiritual renewal and an attitude of giving thanks in everything.

RENEWAL ACTIVITIES

1. Count Your Blessings Game: Divide the class into groups; call out a category and give them 30 seconds to list as many blessings as they can think of in that particular area. Mark out the ones listed more than once and see which group has the most left. Call out a different category for each round.

2. Have men volunteer to lead the class in prayers of thanksgiving.

7

RENEW YOUR FOCUS
"Spiritual ADD"

Attention Deficit Disorder (ADD) is a neurobiologically based developmental disability with three main symptoms: inattention, hyperactivity and impulsivity. It is said to affect 3 percent to 5 percent of all people and can seriously interfere with one's ability to function. In contrast, spiritual ADD is far more widespread. This destructive disorder is not physically or chemically based but results from inattentiveness to the central message of God's Word. Christians suffering from this malady are easily distracted from God's primary purpose for their lives and have difficulty focusing on the fundamentals of Christian living. The answer is not medication but meditation.

> ◆
>
> **Encouragement
> for Renewal**
>
> *If I am to enjoy
> spiritual renewal,
> I must renew
> my focus.*

Both ADD and spiritual ADD are aggravated by the complex fast-changing culture in which we live. A person can become overwhelmed by the vast amounts of information available today. Data asphyxiation, being smothered by facts, figures and various forms of sensory stimuli, can contribute to the complications of either condition. Satan has not hesitated to use the technological developments of our time to sidetrack saints into a tiresome preoccupation with minutiae. He is not content to sit by and watch them concentrate on more inspiring themes of the Gospel. All of God's Word must be honored, but there is no question that some parts carry greater weight than others (Matthew 23:23). Life is full of requirements that call for close attention. In fact, the demands of school or work or managing a home can often seem exhausting if not crushing. Some people feel the same way about the requirements of God. The 66 books of the Bible intimidate many people. That uneasy feeling grows when they think of additional aids such as commentaries, dictionaries and lexicons written to help them understand the Bible. Information overload can be discouraging even for dedicated Christians. There is so much to learn that people often despair of the possibility of knowing how to please God. They think only a few superhuman spiritual scholars can attain to it.

The Lord knew that all men and women would feel this way on some days. That is why in the midst of imparting instructions to Israel He provided a single sentence describing His will for man. That message is boiled down into a concentrated form that any spiritual-minded person can understand: "And now, Israel, what does the Lord your God require of you, but to fear the Lord your God, to walk in all His ways and to love Him, to serve the Lord your God with all your heart and with all your soul and to keep the commandments of the Lord and His statutes which I command you today for your good?" (Deuteronomy 10:12-13). These five requirements summarize man's duty before God:

- Fear the Lord,
- Walk in His ways,
- Love Him,
- Serve Him with all your heart and soul,
- Keep the commandments.

In other words, God wants His creation to love and respect Him and express that in a lifestyle of obedient service. Although the details of God's expectations are by no means unimportant, this concise statement makes them less intimidating. As one moves in the right direction – learning, growing, maturing, becoming – the heavenly Father can and will be pleased.

Fear the Lord

The first of man's basic duties is to fear the Lord. This kind of fear is positive and beneficial. Anything that dwarfs man by its magnitude can incite a sense of awesome fear. Just think about how it feels to stand at the foot of a mountain or on the shore of a seemingly boundless ocean or to look up at the virtual limitlessness of space. That sense of awe is multiplied when contemplating the One who made all of these things. God's wisdom and power and love are on display throughout the universe, declaring His worthiness to receive man's reverence and praise.

Fear is also beneficial because it restrains sinful tendencies. When a person knows he will stand in judgment before so great a Being, it produces a healthy respect for God that has a powerful influence on behavior (Hebrews 10:31). Truly, "The fear of the Lord is the beginning of wisdom" (Proverbs 9:10).

Walk in His Ways

The command to walk in God's ways portrays man's earthly existence as a journey down a pathway leading to eternity. A person should develop a lifestyle that reflects a living relationship with God. Every human being must choose to travel one of two roads in life: the way of man or the way of God. That choice is made evident by all that a person says and does.

Jeremiah prayed, "O Lord, I know the way of man is not in himself: It is not in man who walks to direct his own steps" (Jeremiah 10:23). This sentiment was paralleled in the book of Proverbs: "There is a way that seems right to man, But its end is the way of death" (Proverbs 14:12). Despite these warnings, many people continue to reject God's ways when dealing with questions of religious faith and morality.

Jesus explained the appeal of man's way by describing it as a broad road, easy and enjoyable to travel. In the end, though, it invariably leads to destruction (Matthew 7:13-14). God's way, in contrast, is pictured as narrow and difficult; yet without exception, it ultimately leads to joy in heaven. The point is that the path of least resistance is seldom the right choice in life. God's way is definitely more challenging, but it is also more rewarding every time.

Using Moses' analogy of life as a path, Paul enthusiastically challenged every Christian to walk by faith and not by sight (2 Corinthians 5:7). Walking by sight refers to ordering life by man's limited wisdom without the aid of divine revelation. To walk by faith suggests a person will trust God and follow His instructions recorded in the Bible. Like Enoch (Genesis 5:22) and Noah (6:9), all Christians should make walking with God the supreme goal of their lives.

Love Him

The heart of God's will for man is the duty to love Him. But what does it mean to love God? Is it limited to sentimentality, or is there more to loving God than emotional attachment? Although Christian love contains an emotional component, it is not emotion driven. Biblical love is an exercise of the will, not a product of the latest mood. Jesus explained that genuine love for God is best observed in the way one treats fellow human beings. It is a personal commitment to the health and growth of others without regard for whether they respond in kind. It is loving others as God has loved us.

The other requirements listed alongside love in Moses' outline of religious obligations are really just different expressions of hearts filled with love for God. They are dimensions of love like shape, texture, color and fragrance are different qualities of a single flower. Those who genuinely love God revere Him, walk in His ways, serve Him, and obey Him. Real love involves a person's behavior and not just his feelings. Biblical love consists of actions as well as attitude.

Serve Him With All Your Heart and Soul

Serving God is unquestionably a byproduct of love. Paul linked these concepts when he thanked God for the Thessalonians' "labor of love" (1 Thessalonians 1:3) and defined acceptable religion as "faith working through love" (Galatians 5:6). Jesus declared service to be the road to greatness in the kingdom of heaven and backed up His words with His own example (Mark 10:44-45). If a person is serious about pleasing God, he cannot be satisfied sitting on the sideline of life. Because God's love took the form of action so must our own. In the home, local church and neighborhood, the Lord's people should continually cultivate lives of sacrificial service.

Moses said it is vitally important to examine the attitude with which service is rendered. Christians should make it their goal to minister enthusiastically, not begrudgingly. Acceptable service must be performed with all the heart and soul. A genuine interest in people is basic to the biblical concept of servanthood.

Keep the Commandments

Moses ended his summary of God's requirements with the charge to keep the commandments. In brief, love for God requires obedience. That idea is captured in James' exhortation, "But be doers of the word, and not hearers only, deceiving yourselves" (James 1:22).

In the Sermon on the Mount, Jesus declared, "Not everyone who says to Me, 'Lord, Lord,' shall enter the kingdom of heaven, but he who does the will of My Father in heaven" (Matthew 7:21). Jesus and James concur that it is not enough merely to study or agree with God's Word. A person must actually do the Lord's will to enter His kingdom and enjoy the blessings of heaven.

This does not mean that pleasing God is possible only for those who achieve perfection. God knew man would fall short of attaining sinlessness. That is precisely why He provided a Savior through whom forgiveness is possible (1 John 2:1). He realized that even the most conscientious Christian would need His mercy. Thank God for His patience and understanding!

Christians must be careful not to presume upon the grace of God. Some attempt to sidestep the requirement for obedience by minimizing it in light of God's goodness. Obedience is much more than a fringe aspect of the faith (2 Thessalonians 1:7-9; Hebrews 5:9; 1 John 3:6). To downplay its importance as an expression of genuine love and trust is a terrible miscalculation. Although works can never merit salvation, they are nonetheless essential to receive the blessings made possible by Christ's atoning death. Obedience is the instinctive response of bona fide faith.

An important part of spiritual renewal is stepping back and taking a fresh look at the big picture of God's will for your life. Details are important, but they should be understood as amplifications of more basic axioms of the faith. God's requirements are challenging but not unreasonable or impossible. The highest aim of life should always be to please the heavenly Father. Fear Him, walk in His ways, love Him, serve Him, and obey Him. Yes, you can do that!

DISCUSSION

1. Have you ever thought that it was impossible to please God? Why? Have you changed your mind?

2. What does it mean to fear God?

3. Share a time when you were filled with a sense of awe at God's greatness.

4. Why does God qualify the requirement of service with the words "all your heart and soul" (Deuteronomy 10:12-13)?

5. How can we walk with God today?

6. What does loving God mean to you personally?

7. Which of the five basic requirements in Deuteronomy 10:12-13 is the most difficult?

8. What advice would you give someone who is despairing because he or she has fallen short of God's requirements?

9. What is the difference between the demand for obedience and the demand for perfection?

10. How is it possible to abuse the grace of God?

RENEWAL ACTIVITIES

1. The five requirements outlined in today's lesson form the basis of man's fundamental mission in life. Use these criteria to write a personal mission statement of a paragraph or less in length. Ask for volunteers to share with the class.

2. Give thanks to God for the Bible's foundational statements that provide focus and encouragement for struggling saints.

8

RENEW YOUR SINCERITY
"Real Religion"

Faith in Christ should be "effective" not "affected." The Bible warns against having a form of godliness but denying its power (2 Timothy 3:5). Does that describe you? Is your religion one of show or substance? Is your commitment to Christ phony or real? How can a person tell if his religious devotion is genuine or pretend?

The best way to answer that question is through careful self-examination. A person should ask himself, "What difference does my faith make in the way I live my life?" Authentic faith should influence all that one says and does.

Israelites who truly loved God were to show it by steadfastly keeping God's covenant commands. Their faith was to

> **Encouragement for Renewal**
>
> *If I am to enjoy spiritual renewal, I must relate my faith to everyday life.*

be a way of life and not just the performance of an isolated ritual. Moses presented them with a broad range of laws that touched on every aspect of their existence (Deuteronomy 11-25).

Assemblies

There were the expected cultic laws regarding special times and seasons. Proper observance of holy days was an important part of Jewish religious life. Passover, the Feast of Weeks and the Feast of Tabernacles were required assemblies for the men of the nation (Deuteronomy 16:16). Likewise, Christians are commanded not to forsake the assembly of the saints (Hebrews 10:25). These passages indicate that faithfulness in worship is a fundamental part of real religion. Still, there is much, much more.

• *Stewardship.* People must also demonstrate the genuineness of their faith by the use of their money. God required the Israelites to honor Him by supporting the priesthood through tithing (Deuteronomy 14:22). In the New Testament, God's people are commanded to give as they have been prospered (1 Corinthians 16:2) and to do so with cheerful hearts (2 Corinthians 9:7). Paul says that the generous contributions of the Corinthians proved the sincerity of their love for God (2 Corinthians 8:8, 24). The pocketbook is clearly one of the best tests of a person's religion: "For where your treasure is, there your heart will be also" (Matthew 6:21).

• *Submission.* Regular attendance at assemblies of the church and financial support of its ministries do evidence religious devotion. Important as they are, what a person does the rest of the week may be an even better indicator of the real state of his faith. Consider the home for instance. A Jewish son might fancy himself a religious person for having attended the Passover feast, but when he returns home if he stubbornly rebels against his parents, his religion is vain (Deuteronomy 21:18-21). In like fashion, there is no finer way for a Christian teenager to demonstrate spiritual maturity than to honor his parents (Ephesians 6:1-3). What is done in worship one day of the week cannot take the place of a daily walk with God.

• *Faithfulness.* Israel's religion was also tested in the marriage relationship. Faithfulness to one's spouse was equated with faithfulness to God. To commit physical adultery would also be an act of sin against God (Deuteronomy 22:22). Similarly, a Christian's faith must be expressed in sexual purity within marriage (Hebrews 13:4). Husbands (Ephesians 5:25) and wives (Titus 2:4) authenticate their faith in Christ by loving and cherishing one another.

• *Integrity.* Public officials were to fulfill their offices in a manner becoming a member of the covenant community. Israelite kings were not to conduct themselves like their heathen counterparts. They were not to devote themselves to the attainment of personal wealth, power and pleasure (Deuteronomy 17:14-20), nor were they to think of themselves more highly than their brother Israelites. Instead, they were to see themselves as humble servants of God and their nation.

• *Citizenship.* Judges were repeatedly exhorted to carry out their duties with great care. Their religion was to be reflected in fair and impartial judgment (Deuteronomy 16:18-20). To pervert justice or accept a bribe would have rendered their tithes and sacrifices meaningless.

In turn, the people's faith was put to the test by the Lord's demand for honest testimony in court (Deuteronomy 19:15-21). He also insisted that they abide by decisions rendered by the judicial system (17:10-13). Integrity in public office and good citizenship exhibited Israel's genuine faith in God. Likewise, Christians are instructed to subject themselves to governmental powers as a demonstration of covenant loyalty and faith in Christ (Romans 13:1-7).

• *Neighborliness.* Being a good neighbor was perhaps the most basic expression of sincere religion. If an Israelite saw his neighbor's livestock straying, he was not to ignore it. If he knew whose it was, he was to return it (Deuteronomy 22:1-4). If he did not know the owner, then he was to take it home and protect it until the owner came looking for it. The same was to be done with anything a person may have lost.

Jesus taught His followers that it is wrong to neglect a neighbor in distress. In the parable of the good Samaritan (Luke 10:24-37), the Lord defined a man's neighbor as anyone in need. Christians demonstrate the genuineness of their faith by how they treat all people, especially the lowly (Matthew 25:40). Even dealings with enemies can reflect the state of a Christian's relationship with God (5:43-48).

• *Diet.* The covenant required Israelites to eat the right foods as part of their religious devotion (Deuteronomy 14:3). For health reasons, or perhaps to distinguish themselves from the idolatrous nations around them, the Lord's people were to abstain from eating what was "unclean" (v. 7). Paul taught that Christians are no longer under the Mosaical food laws (1 Timothy 4:3-5), yet Christians should still regard what they take into their bodies as a religious matter.

Addictive and destructive drugs such as tobacco and alcohol enslave their users and erode both mental and physical health. The body is entrusted to man for a short time in order to serve God. To destroy it prematurely through self-indulgent behavior would be poor stewardship to say the least. Even healthy food should be consumed only after it has been sanctified by prayer.

• *Dress.* The clothing worn by Israelites was another manifestation of their faith (Deuteronomy 22:5). The covenant forbade transvestism and called upon Israelites to dress in a way that would reflect the natural order as God created it. To obscure the distinctiveness of the sexes could lead to gender confusion with implications ranging from homosexual behavior to the undermining of God ordained roles for men and women in the home and public worship. The New Testament also speaks of clothing as a spiritual concern when Paul urges Christian women to dress modestly and decently (1 Timothy 2:9). Clothing can communicate worldliness (materialism or moral looseness) or godliness.

Moses went on to instruct the Israelites about many other matters such as financial debt, treatment of slaves and respect for animal and plant life. It is amazing just how extensively the covenant reached into their daily activities. In a similar fashion, Paul said that whatever Christians say or do should be done in the name of Jesus (Colossians 3:17). Their words and actions should reflect that Christ reigns in their hearts as Lord.

Spiritual renewal is more than a fuzzy philosophy. It is relating faith to everyday life in a meaningful way. It is internally and externally ordering life by Christ's example and teaching. If a Christian is a law-abiding citizen, a dedicated employee, a good neighbor, and a faithful spouse, then there is good reason to believe his religion is sincere!

DISCUSSION

1. How can ritual be substituted for righteousness?

2. How should real religion be demonstrated in the home?

3. How can clothing reflect a person's faith?

4. How does what one takes into the body speak about spirituality?

5. Describe the kind of neighbor you think a Christian should be.

6. What can public officials do to be held in higher esteem today?

7. What kind of citizen should a Christian be?

8. How can children properly demonstrate the genuineness of their faith?

9. What kind of employee should a Christian be?

10. Is a moral lifestyle final and conclusive evidence of a right relationship with God?

RENEWAL ACTIVITIES

1. Divide into two groups. Have one group make a list of possible proofs of genuine faith. Have the other group compile a list of things that suggest a person's religion is vain. Share your lists.

2. Define the words "hypocrite" and "devout." What is the difference between a hypocrite and a person who tries but fails?

3. Have men volunteer to lead the class in petitioning God's help to live authentic Christian lives.

9

RENEW YOUR BEARINGS
"Learn to Discern"

Being lost is one of life's most unsettling experiences. When a person first realizes he or she is disoriented, the instinctive response is to find a point of reference to recover his bearings. A driver will look for road signs to point the right way. A hiker may look for a landmark, growth on trees, or the direction of the sun. Sailors can turn to the stars to navigate safely.

An important concern is where to turn for spiritual direction. Without a proper point of reference, renewal is impossible. If a person takes his bearings from the wrong source, he may drift further from God instead of drawing closer to Him. Those who seek to chart a course toward heaven must take their heading from the Word of God.

> ### Encouragement for Renewal
>
> *If I am to enjoy spiritual renewal, I must renew my bearings.*

The Israelites who set out from Sinai wandered aimlessly for 40 years because they failed to obey the Lord. A new day was dawning as their descendants confidently accepted the challenge of following God's lead. That confidence was shaken when Israel learned that Moses would not accompany them across the Jordan. For 40 years they had depended on him for guidance and instruction. How would they know God's will in the coming days?

The Canaanites turned to the occult for direction in their lives (Deuteronomy 18:9-14). Moses explained that this was one of the reasons God determined to drive them from the land. The Israelites were charged not to listen to mediums, sorcerers or anyone associated with idolatry in its various forms.

Instead, God would raise up a Prophet to instruct His people. Moses declared, "The Lord your God will raise up for you a Prophet like me from your midst, from your brethren. Him you shall hear" (Deuteronomy 18:15). The authority that guided their lives would distinguish them from all other nations. That principle continues to hold true today.

The Prophet

The ultimate fulfillment of these words is found in Jesus Christ the Son of God (Hebrews 1:1-2). When Philip met the Lord, he searched out his friend Nathaniel and declared, "We have found Him of whom Moses in the law, and also the prophets, wrote – Jesus of Nazareth, the son of Joseph" (John 1:45). Jesus rebuked the unbelieving Jews of Jerusalem saying, "Do not think that I shall accuse you to the Father; there is one who accuses you – Moses, in whom you trust. For if you believed Moses, you believe Me; for he wrote of Me" (5:45-46). In his sermon at the gate called Beautiful, Peter appealed to Moses' words to persuade the people to accept Jesus:

> Repent therefore and be converted, that your sins may be blotted out, so that times of refreshing may come from the presence of the Lord, and that He may send Jesus Christ, who was preached to you before, whom heaven must receive until the times of restoration of all things, which God has spoken by the mouth of all His holy prophets since the world began. For Moses truly said to the fathers, "The Lord your God will raise up for you a Prophet like me from your brethren. Him you shall hear in all things, whatever He says to you. And it shall be that every soul who will not hear that Prophet shall be utterly destroyed from among the people" (Acts 3:19-23).

Moses said concerning the new Prophet like himself, "Him you shall hear." What a joy it must have been for him to witness the fulfillment of his prophecy on the Mount of Transfiguration. In a glorified state, Jesus conversed with Moses and Elijah until a cloud overshadowed the group. A voice came out of the cloud saying, "This is My beloved Son. Hear Him!" (Mark 9:7). Jesus was alone when the haze disappeared. In this dramatic way, God declared that the words of His Son take precedence over both the law and the prophets of the Old Testament.

God's Spokespersons

Apparently, Moses' words had a secondary fulfillment that applied more directly to the time of those who received them (Deuteronomy 18:16-19). When God first delivered the Ten Commandments, the terrified multitude asked that He not speak to them in person (Exodus 20:18-19). The Lord consented to their request and the result was a long line of prophets through whom God revealed His will at pivotal points throughout history.

The word "prophet" means mouthpiece or spokesperson. God revealed His will to certain men who in turn delivered the Lord's commandments to the people. This made them, in effect, the mouthpiece of God. A good example of this process is found in the call of Jeremiah. The Lord touched his mouth and said to him, "Behold, I have put My words in your mouth" (Jeremiah 1:9).

Great prophets appeared on the scene at various times and places. Men such as Samuel and Nathan advised King David of God's will. They were followed by the outstanding duo Elijah and Elisha. Then came the writing prophets whose works make up the books of the Bible known as major and minor prophets.

In the infant church, God revealed His Word through prophets once again. This was a temporary measure until the church matured and inspired writings were collected into a book to guide the people (1 Corinthians 13:8-10). Christians continue to serve as God's mouthpiece to the world although it is the inspired message of the New Testament that carries His authority today.

Every individual will be held accountable for his response to the Word of the Lord. Failure to hear the Prophet is a life and death matter (Acts 3:23). Jesus said, "[F]or if you do not believe that I am He, you will die in your sins" (John 8:24). The disobedient will find the very words they reject serving as their judge on the last day (12:48).

False Prophets

The certainty that false prophets would arise complicated matters further for the Israelites (Deuteronomy 18:22). Those who spoke in the name of other gods were easy to identify. The difficulty was knowing the true prophet from a false one when both claimed to be speaking in the name of the Lord. The people wondered in their hearts, "How shall we know the word which the Lord has not spoken?" (v. 21).

Moses counseled the Israelites not to pay attention to prophets whose predictions did not come to pass. The foretelling of false prophets was a lot like forecasting the weather today. It was guesswork based on inference and conjecture. The true prophet was not merely predicting probable outcomes. Speaking God's Word guaranteed him 100 percent accuracy as compared to his counterparts' spasmodic success.

One may wonder why God would allow false teaching to exist in the first place. The definitive answer was given when Moses declared, "[T]he Lord your God is testing you to know whether you love the Lord your God with all your heart and with all your soul" (Deuteronomy 13:3). This test of true love will continue until the end of time.

Modern truth seekers continue to encounter the same problem that Israel wrestled with: "[H]ow shall we know the word which the Lord has not spoken?" (Deuteronomy 18:21). Because God does not speak out of both sides of His mouth, it is obvious that not everything preached in Jesus' name is actually His word. With so many mixed messages, is it really possible for the average person to know God's will?

Discerning God's Will

God wants all people to be saved and to come to the knowledge of the truth (1 Timothy 2:4). His very nature is comforting assurance that He will not impose an impossible task upon mankind. Discerning the Lord's will is certainly an awesome responsibility, but there is no reason to be discouraged. Jesus promised that the truth can be known and that it has real power to liberate from sin (John 8:32).

Desire is the first essential for knowing God's will. Jeremiah wrote, "And you will seek Me, and find Me, when you search for Me with all your heart" (Jeremiah 29:13). Unfortunately, man's desire is often to prove his own position rather than to know God's will. Only honest open, teachable hearts can receive the implanted word that is able to save souls (James 1:21).

Diligence is the other essential. To know if a teaching is true, one must follow the example of the Bereans who searched the Scripture daily in order to evaluate the preaching of Paul (Acts 17:10-11). Paul advised, "Test all things; hold fast what is good" (1 Thessalonians 5:21).

Those who seek God's approval must be serious students of the Bible (2 Timothy 2:15). Convictions must be based on thorough personal investigation of the inspired, authoritative, inerrant Word of God. Desire and diligence, when coupled with proper methods of Bible study, will produce a fruitful knowledge of God's Word.

Many people have lost their spiritual bearings and are adrift in a sea of religious confusion. Renewal begins with a commitment to discern the will of God through determined study of the New Testament as the reference point for deciding all matters of religious faith and practice. Transformation of heart and life are possible whenever a person surrenders his will to the absolute authority of God.

DISCUSSION

1. Why does God allow false teaching to exist?

2. What sources of authority do people turn to for guidance today?

3. Is it really possible for the average person to know the will of God?

4. Discuss the essentials for understanding God's Word.

5. Explain the meaning of the word "prophet."

6. What was the difference between a false prophet and a true one?

7. Why was it important to listen to the Prophet?

8. How is God's nature evidence that His will can be understood?

9. How was Deuteronomy 18:15 fulfilled initially? Ultimately?

10. In what ways are Christians like prophets? How are they different?

RENEWAL ACTIVITIES

1. Write a brief description of Bible books and have class members identify them.

2. Pray for God to increase your love for His Word as the authoritative guide for life, and praise Him for revealing Himself to us.

3. Pick out some songs about the Word of God, and sing them together.

RENEW YOUR MARRIAGE
"When the Knot Begins to Slip"

The wedding day is a very special event in life. It is not every day that couples hire photographers and caterers. A man may never again wear a tuxedo. A woman may never again spend such a large amount on a dress. A wedding is intended to be an once-in-a-lifetime event. There is no doubt that God planned marriage with permanence in mind.

A group of Pharisees once questioned Jesus about the permanence of marriage. They asked, "Is it lawful for a man to divorce his wife for just any reason?" (Matthew 19:3). Jesus responded, "Have you not read that He who made them at the beginning made them male and female, and said, 'For this reason a man

> **Encouragement for Renewal**
>
> *If I am to enjoy spiritual renewal, I must renew my devotion to my mate.*

shall leave his father and mother and be joined to his wife, and the two shall become one flesh'? So then, they are no longer two but one flesh. Therefore what God has joined together, let not man separate" (vv. 4-6).

Leaving

A person's childhood home is God's training ground for a new relationship that transcends the family of origin. Mothers and fathers should be honored for a lifetime, but after marriage, loyalty belongs above all to one's spouse. Leaving mother and father is essential for a man and woman to bond in the way God planned. When this emotional differentiation does not occur, confusion and conflict will result. Without leaving, there can be no successful cleaving.

Parents who love their children will make sure the apron strings are cut and not just loosely untied. Children should not be abandoned, but every precaution should be taken to avoid interfering with God's work of connecting couples to each other. Doing less is better than more. Asking permission is better than assuming. Abstaining is better than taking sides. Think of the new home as a person. Honor its integrity and protect its sanctity. The parents' responsibility is to support the long-term interests of the home above the short-term interests of a newly married child.

Young couples must assume responsibility in moving toward emotional independence. Appealing to Mom and Dad when attempting to resolve conflict is a mistake. It is a blunder to compare one's spouse to a parent of the same gender. Newlyweds must look to one another to supply their needs and doggedly resist perpetuating parental dependencies that diminish marital intimacy and respect.

Cleaving

By referring back to the beginning of marriage, Jesus showed that God designed it to be a lifetime commitment between a man and a woman. The command for husbands and wives to "be joined" (NKJV) or "cleave" (KJV) to one another is clear. The Hebrew word for cleave means "to glue." Marriage partners are instructed by God to "stick" together as they encounter the adventure of life.

The home is under attack by Satan, and only those who are truly committed will survive. As Jesus said in another connection, a house divided against itself cannot stand (Mark 3:24). When problems arise if a husband and wife blame each other and lash out verbally or physically, the foundation of their marriage begins to crumble. They must unite instead of fight. God asks His people to believe that sticking together and working out problems will lead to the greatest happiness in the long run.

For some people, marriage is little more than a trial-and-error means of finding the perfect partner who will satisfy all their wants. Good marriages are made up of imperfect people who realize that they will get out of a relationship what they put into it. By practicing the fine art of cleaving, a couple can beat the odds and build a life together that will go the distance.

Blending

Jesus also stressed the permanence of marriage when he said that "the two shall become one flesh." The result of being joined or cleaving is a oneness that defies explanation. This joining together is symbolized by the lighting of a unity candle at many wedding ceremonies. It is realized in the blending of two distinct personalities across the span of a lifetime. It is the oneness of body, mind, heart and soul. The idea is not for one partner to become a clone but a complement to the other so that, together, they form a whole.

The Lord then issued a warning to those who would destroy this new creation of God. "Therefore what God has joined together, let not man separate" (Matthew 19:6). Some see these words as addressed to the lawyer or judge who usurps the authority of God and seeks to grant a divorce for a reason other than sexual unfaithfulness. Others consider these words as a stern rebuke to any third party who would attempt to alienate the affections of one marriage partner for another.

Jesus' words also speak to husbands and wives themselves. Most broken marriages separate relationally long before they separate legally. That is not a justification to go ahead with divorce. Two wrongs do not make a right, and divorce makes a difficult situation even more complicated to correct.

Too many couples exist in a state of perpetual apathy. Marriages are living things that require nurturing to thrive. Jesus directs His followers to care deeply about their mates and to treat them with courtesy at all times. Open communication enriches the relationship and romantic gestures keep the courtship alive. Anything less and a marriage is unconsciously being undermined. Although it may never reach the courtroom, such a home will be little more than a marital mausoleum where hopes and dreams have died and been laid to rest. Taking a person for granted is a sure way to kill a relationship. It does not take a deliberate choice to destroy a home. In contrast, it takes a conscious effort to build one!

Can Love Be Commanded?

God's counsel for husbands and wives is to love one another (Ephesians 5:25; Titus 2:4). Unfortunately, it is impossible to control the emotions directly. They are not like light switches that can be flipped on and off at will. The good news is that the kind of love God expects in marriage is not limited to feelings. It is principally a gracious way of treating another person. Not surprising, though, feelings toward a spouse can rapidly improve when behavior toward him or her improves.

It also explains how the Lord could instruct His followers to love their enemies (Matthew 5:43-48). "Enemies" may well describe the relationship between some couples. The answer to such a battlefield atmosphere is to extend the white flag of forgiveness and begin loving one another with an unyielding sacrificial love that does not have to be earned or deserved.

The golden rule should be dusted off and put to use (Matthew 7:12). A tit-for-tat attitude leaves everyone wounded and no one a winner (Romans 12:19-21). It is never too late for God to heal a home unless a husband and wife become so proud and stubborn that they refuse to work at rebuilding their relationship. As long as two people are willing to try, God will help them put their home back on a solid foundation by acting themselves into a better way of feeling.

No Quick Fix

The Pharisees were quick to object to Jesus' insistence on permanence in marriage. Was He not contradicting Moses who commanded Israelite men to give their wives a certificate of divorce when they put them away (Deuteronomy 24:1-5)? Jesus dealt with the apparent discrepancy by explaining that Moses was not instituting or approving divorce. He merely provided direction for regulating a practice that had gone on for some time.

Countless Jewish men had hardened their hearts against their wives and God's will for marriage. Moses made it more difficult for husbands to discard their mates by requiring a bill of divorce. This protected the reputation of innocent women whom others might assume to be adulterous without a written explanation of the cause of the divorce. It also shielded women from a legalistic form of wife-swapping. A man who divorced his wife could not remarry her if she had subsequently married another man (this also sheltered the third party from being used to make a previous husband jealous). If he could never have her back, he would think long and hard about his actions rather than acting impulsively.

Moses permitted divorce begrudgingly and sought to regulate it, but this was not the Lord's original intent. From the beginning, God's ideal for marriage was one man and one woman for a lifetime. Malachi 2:16 states, "For the Lord God of Israel says That He hates divorce."

Jesus explained that anyone who divorces his wife and marries another woman commits adultery (Luke 16:18). The one exception to this rule is if the cause of divorce is sexual unfaithfulness. In light of modern scientific knowledge about sexually transmitted diseases, there are physical as well as emotional reasons why God does not compel the innocent party to hold the marriage together. Still, God does not demand the dissolution of the relationship.

Spiritual Solutions

So what should couples do when the knot begins to slip in their marriage? God asks His people to accept by faith that divorce is not the solution. Malachi stated three times that putting a marriage asunder is an act of heartless treachery (Malachi 2:14-16). The safest and most satisfying course is to begin tenaciously cleaving to whatever is left of the marriage and dedicating it to God. Ask for His help, and work diligently at rebuilding love and trust. Couples who put their faith in God can revive troubled marriages.

Moses provided an interesting insight into building a successful home in Deuteronomy 24:5. For one year after marriage, a man was exempt from military service in order to be at home and cheer up his wife. In modern dating, couples knock themselves out trying to make each other happy. The extent to which this activity continues after the altar will determine the success or failure of the relationship.

At some unnoticed point, husbands and wives often stop trying to bring cheer to each other's lives. They merely exist together in a home void of joy or intimacy. To avoid this failure in marriage, sow the seeds of happiness regularly, and remember – as a man sows, so also shall he reap.

The greatest opportunity for spiritual renewal is right in your own home. Determine to love your mate as Christ loves you. Gracious, sacrificial, agape love is the greatest means to personal happiness. As Paul explained, loving your spouse is really just another way of loving yourself (Ephesians 5:28).

DISCUSSION

1. How can God command husbands and wives to love one another?

2. Explain what you think it means to be "one flesh."

3. How can husbands and wives cleave to one another?

4. Why does God permit divorce in cases of sexual unfaithfulness?

5. Must this option be exercised in every case?

6. Why does Malachi call divorce a form of treachery?

7. In what ways are couples responsible for putting their marriages asunder?

8. How can divorce create more problems than solutions in many situations?

9. Where does faith come into play when a person is considering divorce?

10. Share a special memory of how your spouse cheered you up on one occasion.

RENEWAL ACTIVITIES

1. Break into groups and make a list of the top 10 ways to renew your marriage.

2. Decide something you will do this week to bring happiness to your spouse. Be sure to have couples report in class next week.

3. Pray for God's help to overcome the self-centeredness that robs couples of the joy of marriage.

11

RENEW YOUR HAPPINESS
"Let Happiness Pursue You"

In the Declaration of Independence, Thomas Jefferson wrote that all humans are endowed with certain inalienable rights including life, liberty and the pursuit of happiness. He could not guarantee happiness to Americans, but he recognized the appropriateness of such a quest. Never has this coveted commodity been more sought after than in today's society.

Although people continue to scramble for happiness, the results have been terribly disappointing. For all their efforts, most Americans are still anxious, fearful, worried, guilt ridden and burdened. Why are so few people genuinely happy? Why are so many people hurting? One explanation is that they have failed to learn that happiness cannot be pursued directly. Such a chase evolves into the mere pursuit of pleasure, which is only a mirage of happiness.

> ### Encouragement for Renewal
>
> *If I am to enjoy spiritual renewal, I must renew my concept of happiness.*

The Secret of Happiness

The Israelites were facing this same predicament on the plains of Moab as they prepared to enter Canaan. Moses longed for his people to find happiness in the new land. Just before his death, he shared with them the secret of real and lasting joy: Those who obeyed God would be blessed. Covenant faithfulness was the only path to genuine happiness.

God is the source of life and all that makes it abundant and meaningful (Deuteronomy 30:20). Happiness, therefore, is only possible by remaining in fellowship with the Lord. Anyone who disobeys God is, at that very moment, rejecting his only hope of fulfillment in life. God's covenant commands are not like those of selfish kings who seek to advance their own interests. All of His instructions are prompted by selfless love. Each one is designed to promote the greatest good of His creation. Thus, every act of obedience becomes an avenue of blessing.

As Moses spoke, he pictured the blessings that came through humble obedience as real forces that pursued God's people and overwhelmed them: "And all these blessings shall come upon you and overtake you, because you obey the voice of the Lord your God" (Deuteronomy 28:2). His point was, "Instead of chasing after happiness, why not let it pursue you!" David expressed this sentiment poetically in Psalm 23:6: "Surely goodness and mercy shall follow me All the days of my life." "Follow" does not mean that these blessings lag behind and never catch up, but it is the vigorous idea of being pursued and overtaken by God's goodness and mercy. It is the pleasant surprise experienced by those who put God first in their lives.

Blessings

In Deuteronomy 28:3-6, Moses continued his words about happiness by pointing out the extent of the blessings Israel could look forward to if they remained faithful to God.

The righteous would receive God's favor regardless of whether they were city dwellers or country folks. Their families and businesses would prosper; they could rest assured that the necessities of life would be provided and that the Lord would aid them in every undertaking.

The New Testament is no less emphatic in affirming that God blesses the obedient. Jesus put it this way: "Therefore do not worry, saying, 'What shall we eat?' or, 'What shall we drink?' or, 'What shall we wear?' ... But seek first the kingdom of God and His righteousness, and all these things shall be added unto you" (Matthew 6:31, 33). Christians can count on God to provide the physical necessities of each day. Even more precious is His promise of spiritual blessing (Ephesians 1:3).

Curses

The Israelites rejoiced in Moses' encouraging words, but their mood must have changed as he continued. Moses explained that the covenant had a negative as well as a positive side. With a frightening list of curses, he warned the people about the disaster of disobedience. Deuteronomy 28 mentions four times as many curses as blessings. Just as surely as happiness would follow submission, tragedy would result from defiance or neglect.

In actuality, no one but Christ will ever keep the requirements of the law perfectly (Romans 3:23). For that reason, those who base their hope of salvation on flawless compliance with the law merely fall under the curse of the law. In his letter to the Galatians, Paul explained how mankind has been redeemed from this condemnation.

Using Deuteronomy 21:23 (cursed is everyone who is hanged on a tree) Paul showed how Christ made salvation possible by becoming a curse for man (Galatians 3:13; 4:5). When Jesus was nailed to the cross, He took the place of sinners so that, through the gospel, they can be delivered from wrath and showered with blessings from on high. Although humans cannot earn their eternal salvation (Ephesians 2:8-10), they must demonstrate their faith through obedience to receive the benefits made possible by Christ's death at Calvary.

God Knows Best

The heavenly Father asks men and women to believe that, as Creator, He knows best what produces true happiness in life. Foolishly, people continue to look for satisfaction in all the wrong places. Why do people take drugs? Why do they cheat on their spouses? Why are there so many divorces? Why are insider trading, embezzlement and other forms of greed so widespread?

Satan has successfully convinced mankind that sex, money and pleasure are the keys to happiness. Sin does produce its own kind of enjoyment, but it is never as fulfilling as the devil would have one believe (Hebrews 11:25). The long-term consequences are devastating. Guilt, shame, disease and incarceration are not much fun. In contrast, the fruits of virtue and morality are more rewarding every time.

The greatest source of happiness will always be a right relationship with God through His Son, Jesus Christ. The Beatitudes teach that the basis of happiness or blessedness is putting away worldly standards and living a life built on the values of heaven. The Lord wants every person to be happy and has shown how to have such a life. Covenant renewal is the key. The choice is yours (Deuteronomy 30:15-20).

DISCUSSION

1. What is your personal definition of happiness?

2. Is it wrong to pursue happiness?

3. What are some signs of America's headlong pursuit of happiness?

4. Explain the phrase, "Pleasure is only a mirage of happiness."

5. Do you think most people are happy or unhappy? Why?

6. Is it really possible to be happy today? How?

7. Is it possible to have happiness outside of a relationship with God?

8. How can it be said that happiness is a choice?

9. Why do you think there are four times as many curses as blessings in Deuteronomy 28?

10. Explain what it means to let happiness pursue you.

RENEWAL ACTIVITIES

1. Write the Ten Commandments on a chalkboard. Next, make a list of what happens when you obey the underlying principle behind each command. Finally, write down the negative things that can happen when a person disregards each of the commands.

2. Have men lead the class in prayers of thanksgiving to God for the blessing of genuine happiness He alone makes possible.

12

RENEW YOUR FAITHFULNESS
"The Secret Things"

Human beings love secrets and especially to be told a secret. On the other hand, it can be frustrating to know that others have special knowledge to which you are not privileged. Governments and businesses have secrets, as do families and friends. Even God has secrets!

Part of growing up is learning to live with limited knowledge in certain areas of life. Children cannot bear having others know something they will not tell. Mature people can accept not knowing some things and are able to function perfectly well with the information available to them. In His wisdom, God knows some things He has chosen not to reveal at this time. Christians must trust that the knowledge God has provided is adequate to meet their needs and learn to live thankfully and faithfully with the information at hand. Moses issued a similar challenge to the Israelites on the plains of Moab.

**Encouragement
for Renewal**

*If I am to enjoy
spiritual renewal,
I must renew my
respect for the secret
things of God.*

The book of Deuteronomy, and especially chapter 29, was an appeal to covenant faithfulness. Moses began by reminding the Israelites of the blessings God had showered upon them to bring them to the present moment. The Lord's graciousness provided a powerful incentive for Israel to remain faithful to the covenant that bound them to God. Peace and prosperity in the new land hinged on their keeping that agreement. The final verse of the chapter provided the key for averting the national catastrophe that would occur if they were to forget the Lord: "The secret things belong to the Lord our God, but those things which are revealed belong to us and to our children forever, that we may do all the words of this law" (Deuteronomy 29:29). By keeping the covenant and teaching it to their children, they could enjoy His favor without interruption.

The specifics of Israel's future were for God alone to know, but this much was certain – obedience brings blessing. God spelled out two things in the covenant. First, He made His expectations as plain as possible so that every Israelite would know how to please Him. Second, He promised that those who do what He asked would be blessed by conforming to His will. To speculate beyond this would be presumptuous and precarious. Today as then, heaven's blessings rest upon those who seek to know and do the revealed will of God.

Sufficient Knowledge

Moses made it clear that God never intended to give total knowledge to mankind. Nonetheless, the Lord has provided His people with sufficient knowledge. Even those who live in the glorious age when the mystery of the gospel has been revealed must admit that numerous questions remain unanswered. Many secret things still belong only to the Lord, yet God promises there is no reason for discouragement. Ample knowledge has been provided to guide men and women safely through their pilgrimage on earth.

Peter declared that God has provided people with everything they need to know about life and godliness (2 Peter 1:3). Although it is not possible to know everything, the big issues have been settled. How to go to heaven and how to live a God-honoring life are clearly set forth in Scripture. Paul also affirmed the sufficiency of the Bible as a spiritual guide in his second letter to Timothy (3:15-17). The Bible has the power to make believers complete and to equip them thoroughly for every good work. The apostles of the church agreed that it is possible to know God and please Him without knowing everything. Therefore, inexhaustible knowledge cannot be a prerequisite of spiritual renewal.

Sources of Knowledge

What can be known about God is possible because He chose to reveal it. The psalmist proclaimed, "The heavens declare the glory of God; And the firmament shows His handiwork" (Psalm 19:1). The fact that God exists is clearly revealed in nature. Paul says, "For since the creation of the world His invisible attributes are clearly seen, being understood by the things that are made, even His eternal power and Godhead" (Romans 1:20). By carefully observing the universe, it becomes increasingly evident that a loving, wise and powerful Creator is behind it all.

The fact that God chose to reveal Himself further is a magnificent display of divine love. The Hebrew writer declared, "God who at various times and in various ways spoke in time past to the fathers by the prophets, has in these last days spoken to us by His Son" (Hebrews 1:1). God's special revelation to Moses made it possible for Israel to have a personal relationship with Him. The fact that God spoke and disclosed His mind to mortals has forever changed the course of history.

Moses warned the Israelites that it was not their prerogative to go beyond what was written. The secret things were the Lord's and not for man's speculation (Deuteronomy 12:32; Proverbs 14:12; Revelation 22:18). When man presumes to know what God did not reveal, sin is often close behind. Tampering with God's Word was prohibited: "You shall not add to the word which I command you, nor take from it, that you may keep the commandments of the Lord your God which I command you" (Deuteronomy 4:2). If the Israelites deviated from the words of the covenant, they would suffer the consequences of disobedience.

The same principle holds true for Christians. Paul warned that some people would attempt to pervert the gospel (Galatians 1:6-9). Peter spoke of men unlearned and unstable who twist the Scriptures to their own destruction (2 Peter 3:16). John taught, "Whoever transgresses and does not abide in the doctrine of Christ does not have God" (2 John 9). When it comes to matters of religious faith and practice, saints must remain on the safe ground of revelation. The pertinent question is "What has God revealed in the New Testament regarding how people may please Him?"

What Has God Revealed About Salvation?

The most important revelation ever received by mankind was the good news of a Savior. The angels revealed His arrival on earth. John the Baptist revealed Him to be the Lamb of God who takes away the sins of the world. The apostles revealed that the message of His death, burial and resurrection is God's power to save men. There is only one Savior, and His name is Jesus (Acts 4:12). Those who place their hope of salvation in any other will be eternally disappointed (John 14:6).

The Bible also reveals the conditions upon which Christ's work on the cross will save those who are lost in sin. Faith is the most fundamental part of the plan of salvation and is often used as a general term to represent all the steps that follow (Romans 1:16-17). Repentance is revealed to be another essential part of conversion (Acts 3:19). Like faith, it is sometimes used to represent the entire process, but it should never be considered the only condition of forgiveness. Confession is a third necessary requirement (Romans 10:10). If a person expects Jesus to confess Him before the Father, he must also confess Jesus before men (Matthew 10:32-33). God reveals that baptism completes the steps of salvation and serves as the climactic point at which He delivers man from past sin (Mark 16:16).

The subject of baptism has long been controversial among religious people. Christians should base their beliefs about baptism on what is taught in the Bible. The Bible reveals that the mode of baptism is immersion in water. Matthew 3:13-17 and Acts 8:36-39 show the subject of baptism going down into and coming up out of the water. John 3:23 says that baptism requires much water as would be needed for immersion. Romans 6:4-5 and Colossians 2:12 call baptism a burial, implying that it requires a complete covering. Dictionaries that give the meaning of Greek words as they were used in the first century define baptism as immersion.

The Bible also reveals the meaning of baptism. Every conversion story includes baptism as an integral part of the conversion process, and the immediacy of immersion in these accounts confirms that something vital is taking place. The word is found in a context of spiritual urgency throughout the New Testament. Paul linked it with putting on Christ (Galatians 3:26-27) and experiencing newness of life (Romans

6.4). Peter connected it with remission of sins (Acts 2:38) and salvation (1 Peter 3:21). Others associated it with washing away sin (Acts 22:16) and gaining entrance into the kingdom of God (John 3:5). These passages leave no doubt as to the importance of baptism.

What Has God Revealed About the Church?

The church of Christ is also revealed in the Bible and can be identified today by the same features described in the New Testament. The model church was organized with elders overseeing autonomous congregations (Acts 14:23; Titus 1:5). The terms "bishop," "shepherd," "pastor" and "presbyter" are synonymous with elder and refer to the same work. Any form of church government other than a plurality of elders over independent congregations is supplementary to what God revealed.

The church of the Bible had a distinct form of worship as well. They sang psalms, hymns and spiritual songs while making melody in their hearts (Ephesians 5:19; Colossians 3:16). No man-made instruments are mentioned in the worship of the early church, and history confirms their absence for hundreds of years. Praising God was done exclusively through the human voice, and primitive song services featured congregational singing.

Luke mentions several avenues of worship in addition to singing (Acts 2:47). When Christians gathered, they enjoyed rich fellowship while prayers were lifted to heaven and God's Word was fervently proclaimed. Each first day of the week, they partook of the Lord's Supper, sometimes referred to in Scripture as the breaking of bread (20:7; 1 Corinthians 11:17-29).

These people were first called Christians at Antioch, and that revealed name has been precious to the followers of Christ ever since (Acts 11:26). A term of derision to unbelievers, it was a badge of honor to those who put their faith in Jesus. Those who wear Christ's name should live holy lives patterned after the Lord's example and teaching recorded in the Bible.

What God revealed to the apostles, they in turn delivered to the church. That body of teaching was so sacred it became known as "the faith." Its message was so vital that a New Testament epistle was written to urge Christians to defend it against anyone who would change or corrupt it (Jude 3). Contending for the faith means upholding New Testament Christianity both in spirit and in form. Simply put, spiritual renewal means going back to the Bible.

DISCUSSION

1. Why has God not revealed everything He knows?

2. How has God revealed Himself to mankind? Is this knowledge sufficient for man's needs?

3. What does God's revelation say about His love for humanity?

4. What has God revealed about a Savior?

5. What has God revealed about salvation from past sins?

6. What has God revealed about baptism?

7. What has God revealed about New Testament worship?

8. What has God revealed about the government of the church?

9. What has God revealed about interpersonal relationships and individual morality?

10. What kinds of problems are created when someone goes beyond what God has revealed and presumes upon the secret things of God?

RENEWAL ACTIVITIES

1. If you could ask God one question, what would it be? Have each person write down what he or she would like to ask. Does God's Word address many of these questions by principle if not directly? Can a person please God and go to heaven if his or her question cannot be answered at this time?

2. Spend time in prayer thanking God for the love He showed by revealing Himself and allowing us to have a personal relationship with Him. Express thanks for the sufficient knowledge He has provided.

13

RENEW YOUR PEACE
"The Everlasting Arms"

As the Israelites prepared to enter Canaan, they were filled with mixed emotions. They knew the land was fertile and prosperous, but gaining control of it would be difficult. For 40 years, they depended on the leadership of Moses to bring them through the wilderness. Now, as the challenge of conquering Canaan stood before them, they had to come to grips with the news that Moses would accompany them no further. Imagine their anxiety as they anticipated life without their famous leader.

God would not permit Moses to lead the nation into the new land because of a sin he committed during the wilderness wandering (Numbers 20:1-13). At Meribah, the people quarreled with Moses and Aaron because there was no water to drink. The brothers retreated to the tent of meeting to ask for God's help and received special instructions for miraculously bringing water from a rock.

> ◆
> ### Encouragement for Renewal
>
> *If I am to enjoy spiritual renewal, I must renew my confidence in God's providential care.*

Instead of speaking to the rock as he was told, Moses struck the rock with his staff and spoke harshly to the Israelites: "Hear now, you rebels!

Must we bring water for you out of this rock?" (Numbers 20:10). Because he did not honor the Lord in the sight of the people, he forfeited his right to be among those entering Canaan. Moses pleaded with God to reconsider, but the Lord had made up His mind (Deuteronomy 3:25-26). The matter was settled, and Moses was commanded not to bring it up again.

The finality of God's response must have broken Moses' heart. His concern was not merely for himself. Like a father who longs to help his child through one of life's troublesome milestones, he wanted to help the children of Israel through the difficult task before them.

Moses could sense the Israelites' uneasiness and sought to comfort their troubled hearts. In the past, they had looked to his strong and sure arms for help. Now he reminded them of One far greater than himself: "The eternal God is your refuge, And underneath are the everlasting arms" (Deuteronomy 33:27). In reality, God had sustained them all along.

Moses' words to Israel are as relevant today as when they were first spoken. Like the Israelites, Christians need encouragement in the face of life's struggles. Enduring comfort can be found in Moses' message of hope.

Underneath

Consider the word "underneath." All people long to know the underlying meaning of life. According to Moses, life is undergirded by the promise of God's providential care, and pleasing Him is the purpose beneath man's earthly existence.

The plight of the Israelites appeared utterly hopeless without their capable leader Moses. They realized they needed support and strength beyond themselves. Moses' assured them that God would be present to bear them up in every challenge they would face.

Life can seem just as impossible today. God's people are often frightened by the future and terrified by their own weaknesses. Each day can seem like walking a tightrope stretched between heaven and earth. Just as a high-wire performer wants the security of a net below him, man desperately longs for something underneath.

Arms

All of humanity can rejoice in Moses' assurance that underneath are the everlasting arms. "Arms" implies personhood – not just something but someone to undergird life – a living, conscious, powerful being to care personally for those He loves.

Because God is spirit, these arms can only be seen by faith. Although they are not physical or fleshly, they are real and strong just the same. This is the Holy Spirit's way of conveying to finite human minds something about the nature of God. He is saying that when someone contemplates all the good that is done by the strength of human arms, God is able to do even more through His own divine means.

Young children look to the sturdy dependable arms of a mother or father to care for their needs. How much more supportive and secure are the arms of the heavenly Father when caring for His spiritual children. He knows when they are afraid or heartbroken or in danger or in need. Oh, yes! There is something underneath: the everlasting arms of God.

Everlasting

The power of God's arms is wonderfully expressed in the superlative "everlasting." In Job 40:9 the question was raised, "Have you an arm like God?" These are no ordinary arms, and it is thrilling to contemplate their excellencies.

Why are they everlasting? Because they will never tire! Through eternity, they will not weaken. The psalmist has declared, "Even from everlasting to everlasting, You are God" (Psalm 90:2). In contrast, recall the scene when Israel did battle with Amalek at Rephidim (Exodus 17:8-16). While Joshua fought the battle below, Moses stood on a nearby hilltop with his arms stretched out toward heaven as an appeal for help. As long as his arms were held high, Israel was victorious, but as he tired and his arms began to droop, they were put on the defensive. Had it not been for Aaron and Hur holding up Moses' arms, Israel would have been soundly defeated that day. How much better are God's arms than those of the greatest mortals! No load is too great for these tireless arms. Peter knew this and encouraged weary saints to cast all their care upon God (1 Peter 5:7). With God's help, no earthly burden is too great to bear. Sometimes it appears that a problem is too big to solve or too complicated to cope with. Moses understood that feeling, but 120 years of experience told him nothing was too hard for the Lord.

A third reason God's arms are called everlasting is because it is impossible to outgrow them. David said, "When my father and my mother forsake me, Then the Lord will take care of me " (Psalm 27:10). The time comes when children outgrow the arms of their parents who must eventually pass from this life and leave them alone to face the world. It is not so with God. From childhood into adolescence, and from adulthood into old age, His powerful arms are always there.

Consoling Arms

Knowing the everlasting arms are underneath provides the confidence needed to face life courageously. It also gives courage when facing the death of a loved one. As the Israelites grieved over the passing of Moses, they remembered his words about God's providential care and found the strength they needed to carry on. Christians can count on the same help and solace when entrusting their departed loved ones to the compassionate arms of their Creator.

Moses' words are equally comforting when confronting the prospect of one's own death. As Moses contemplated the everlasting arms sustaining him throughout life, he calmly ascended Mount Pisgah knowing they were beneath him yet (Deuteronomy 34:1-7). Although he was sure he would not return, he trusted those arms to carry him to a far better land. After drinking in a breathtaking view of Canaan, his life ended and his spirit returned to the arms of its Maker. Confidence in God's providence makes it possible to face death with courage and composure. That is why David could boast, "Yea, though I walk through the valley of the shadow of death, I will fear no evil. For You are with me" (Psalm 23:4). He will do no less for His children today.

Whatever burdens one must bear, whatever temptations one may wrestle with, whatever struggles life may bring, the everlasting arms of God will always be there. Those arms are outstretched to you even now. Spiritual renewal is the consequence of returning His embrace and trusting in His continual presence.

DISCUSSION

1. Why did Moses call God's arms everlasting?

2. How do God's arms provide courage to deal with life's difficulties?

3. How do they provide encouragement when a loved one dies?

4. How do they give a person the courage to face his own death?

5. Why was it necessary for Moses to remind Israel of God's providence?

6. Why did the Holy Spirit choose the word "arms" if God is spirit?

7. What did Moses mean when he said God's arms are "underneath"?

8. How is it possible for our arms to act as arms of God undergirding the lives of others?

9. What is the connection between the covenant and God's providence?

10. How does confidence in God's providence promote spiritual renewal?

RENEWAL ACTIVITIES

1. Share something you found renewing during your study of Deuteronomy.

2. How will you continue the renewal process now that you have finished the book?

Simple Steps

for

RENEWING YOUR SPIRITUAL LIFE

Renew your covenant relationship with God.

Renew your absolute trust in God.

Renew your core values.

Renew your wholehearted commitment.

Renew your devotion to family.

Renew your gratitude.

Renew your attention to basics.

Renew your application of faith to everyday life.

Renew your spiritual bearings.

Renew your devotion to your mate.

Renew your concept of happiness.

Renew your respect for the secret things of God.

Renew your confidence in God's providential care.

AFTERWORD

Many writings on the subject of spiritual renewal can be more discouraging than helpful. They portray spiritual growth as a complex, mystical experience beyond the reach of average Christians. My hope is that this book aids you in putting to rest these myths regarding sanctification. Although challenging, God's plan for renewing your spiritual life is simple and straightforward. Increase your love for God and increase your determination to abide by His Word. That is the path to blessing.

> Trust and obey,
> For there's no other way,
> To be happy in Jesus,
> But to trust and obey.

SPIRITUAL RENEWAL SURVEY

1. What does spiritual renewal mean to you?

2. Which of these sentences best describes your spiritual life at the present time?
    a. I really feel good about it.
    b. I'm struggling right now.
    c. I am on the verge of losing it.
    d. I don't have one anymore.

3. What part of your life most needs renewing?
    a. My attitude
    b. My speech
    c. My character
    d. My service
    e. My knowledge
    f. My worship
    g. My relationships
    h. My priorities
    i. My values
    j. My devotional life
    k. My _____
    l. Everything

4. Do you believe spiritual renewal is really possible for you?
    a. No. I'm too weak, and I've failed too many times.
    b. Yes. All things are possible with God's help.

5. How committed are you to renewing your spiritual life?
    a. I know I need to, but I'm just too busy right now.
    b. I will make the time. It is that important.

6. Name some things you find personally renewing.

7. What are some common hindrances to spiritual renewal?

8. What danger is there in equating renewal with perfection?

9. What do you hope to get out of class this quarter?

10. What will be most satisfying about renewing your spiritual life?